ENTERING THE CAVE OF THE HEART

ENTERING THE CAVE OF THE HEART

Eastern Ways of Prayer for Western Christians

by
Kathleen Healy, RSM

PAULIST PRESS
New York/Mahwah

Acknowledgements

The publisher gratefully acknowledges the permission of The National Biblical Catechetical and Liturgical Centre, Bangalore, India, for the use of *Praying Seminar*, edited by D.S. Amlorpavadoss, and The Vedanta Society of Southern California for the use of the excerpt from *The Sermon on the Mount According to Vedanta* by Swami Prabhavananda.

Library of Congress Cataloging-in-Publication Data

Healy, Kathleen.
    Entering the cave of the heart.

    Bibliography: p.
    1. Spiritual life.   2. Prayer.   3. Christianity and other religions—Hinduism.   4. Hinduism—Relations—Christianity.   I. Title.
BL624.H38   1986   248.3   86-5012
ISBN 0-8091-2792-X (pbk.)

Published by Paulist Press
997 Macarthur Boulevard
Mahwah, New Jersey 07430

Printed and bound in the
United States of America

Contents

Introduction   1

PART ONE:
EASTERN PATHS TO GOD FOR CHRISTIANS

I.   Why Eastern Ways of Prayer?   5

II.   Love, Service, Wisdom: The Three Margas   44

III. A Road to Contemplation: Yoga   57

IV.   A Buddhist Way of Meditation: Vipassana   82

V.   Scriptural Prayer: The Bible and the Upanishads   91

VI.   Prayer Through Art: Symbol and Icon   108

VII. Ashram Prayer: Christian and Hindu   118

PART TWO:
EASTERN PRACTICES OF PERSONAL AND
GROUP PRAYER FOR CHRISTIANS

I.	Prayer of the Name: Namjapa	129
II.	Prayer in Music and Song: Bhajan	142
III.	Prayer at Daybreak: Samdhya	148
IV.	Prayer for Light: Deepavali	154
V.	Prayer for All Human Beings: Pongal	160
VI.	Prayer of Silence: Gandhian Maun	167
VII.	The Lord's Prayer: A Hindu Reflection	171
	Glossary	179
	Selected Bibliography	187

We are living through the greatest crisis in the history of the world; and the crisis is centered precisely in the country that has made a fetish out of action and has lost (or perhaps never had) the sense of contemplation. Far from being irrelevant, prayer, meditation, and contemplation are of the utmost importance in America today.

Thomas Merton
Contemplation in a World of Action

Introduction

While remaining always true to the essential message of the Gospel, Christians in the United States are opening themselves more and more to "all that is true and holy" in the great Oriental religions (Vatican II). Harmonization of Eastern and Western paths of prayer offer hope that the invincible force of love will draw all women and men to completion in Christ.

Entering the Cave of the Heart is an outgrowth of more than two years' experience of Eastern spirituality in India, Burma, Thailand, and Japan, as well as six years of study of ecumenical dialogue between Western Christians and Indians. As a Fulbright Professor at the University of Madras, South India, and later as a research scholar in the East, I interviewed more than one hundred and twenty-five Eastern spiritual leaders—Hindu, Buddhist, and Christian. I became aware of the growing spiritual exchange between East and West, particularly between Christians and Hindus.

Part One is a commentary on Eastern paths to God as a help to Western Christians in prayer, meditation, and contemplation, with practical guides. Part Two offers models of Eastern practices of personal and group prayer for Christians. The union of the profound interiority characteristic of the East with the active apostolic love and service of neighbor distinctive of the West is an integrative force in the life of many American Christians today.

I am grateful to the many theologians, philosophers, swamis, gurus, and women and men religious with whom I have studied and prayed in both East and West. I will not forget the spiritual insight of the following: Dom Bede Griffiths, Shantivanam Ashram, Tamil Nadu, South India; Raimundo Panikkar, Varanasi, Uttar Pradesh, North India, and the University of California, Santa Barbara; D.S. Amalorpavadoss, Chairman of the Department of Christianity, University of Mysore, South India, and Acharya of Anjoli Ashram, Mysore; and the late Abhishiktananda (Dom Henri le Saux), who died in North India in 1976.

My gratitude is due to my religious congregation, the Pittsburgh Sisters of Mercy, and to the administrative officers of Salve Regina College, Newport, Rhode Island, where I worked on the manuscript as a Visiting Professor. Finally, I am indebted to my editor, Robert Hamma, of Paulist Press, New Jersey.

One

EASTERN PATHS TO GOD
FOR CHRISTIANS

I

Why Eastern Ways of Prayer?

—————————

1. Spiritual Search of the Western Christian Today

Today many Christians in the West are becoming aware that we have been too long content with a form of prayer which scarcely goes beyond words, devotional practices, and meditation defined as a thought process. Some of us have discovered that the age-old ideal of true contemplation, of direct experience of God in prayer, has been almost lost to us. We reflect, moreover, that we have sometimes been satisfied with a theology based on reason alone which does not lead us to communion with God in the Spirit. Instinctively, we come to realize that reason alone, even when enlightened by faith, does not always lead us inevitably to union with God, that we must seek the Spirit within our own hearts, the center of our being.[1]

Christians sometimes ask themselves whether it is enough

to keep the commandments and to serve their neighbors. We recall with a certain uneasiness that the Gospel calls us first of all to love God himself with all our heart and soul and mind and strength. Scripture calls us to a love of God which surpasses all knowledge. This first and greatest commandment, we come to discover through personal experience, is a call to contemplation. This experience of God is not an idea; it is a reality within the human heart. Many Western Christians therefore are seeking not words about God but experience of God. We are coming to realize that, while the demands to help our sisters and brothers in Christ are greater than ever before in history, our love and service of others is void and empty without deep inward union with Christ in the Spirit.

As pilgrims on the frontier of the known and unknown in the late twentieth century, we Christians sometimes find ourselves helpless and lost without experience of the sacred. Everyday life teaches us that love of others is ineffective without reciprocal contemplation and service within our own lives. Holiness, communion with God, cannot be feigned. A good person reveals herself or himself not just by action but by simple presence. Witness is far more than words; indeed, witness is never words alone. Holiness is both being and doing. A person's interior union with God is inevitably manifest to others. In the mystery of grace, one who lives in the Spirit often leads others to God without apparent effort, for Christ lives and acts in those who seek continual union with him.

Many Western Christians today, through relationships with Easterners formerly impossible to them, have become aware that contemplation, the experience of God within the center of one's being, is the deepest intuition of the Eastern soul. Young people of Europe and America have discovered this truth in their experiences in the East, particularly in India. It is a fact that the youth culture of today in the West, in spite of their insistence on immediacy of experience of the material world here and now, are in search of a breakthrough to God. Young people long for experience of God within the framework of a simple life. Hundreds of young Western women and men turn to India today, seeking a basic interior life as a way to find God. We discover them sitting on the ground in Hindu or Christian ashrams, listening to spiritual teachers, searching for the Spirit within their own hearts. We ask why they are turning to the spirituality of Eastern civilization.

Unfortunately, it is often thought that these young Christians have abandoned their faith. The truth is that they are reacting against a particular form of believing, a particular way of prayer. They have sometimes identified their prayer and early relationships to God with certain religious practices, formulas, and rituals which exist parallel to but somehow separate from their daily lives. Thus their prayer and worship have seemed to them to be lifeless and empty. Western youth, in their turning to the East, are perhaps telling Christians something significant about themselves.

The famous Hindu guru, Swami Ramana Maharishi, had hundreds of faithful followers who learned from him how to seek God. He willingly spoke with anyone who was searching for experience of God simply and sincerely, but he had no interest in people who displayed their status or learning. Indeed he loved best to talk with shepherds he met in his home in the hills of southeast India.

One day a famous university scholar approached him and declared, "Master, we poor ignoramuses are seeking the path of truth everywhere in vain. I have read all the Scriptures, I have studied all the philosophers, from Descartes to Russell. Whom should I follow?" Maharishi remained silent. After a few minutes, the pedant began to show off his learning, finally begging, "Swami, for God's sake, tell me which way I should go!" And the holy man answered simply, "Go back the way you came."[2]

The sincere Western Christian today feels more and more a need for inward recollection and contemplation. Experience of the devastating *absence* of contemplation is perhaps more profound in the West, however, than a conscious need for it. When Western Christians suddenly come in touch with the Eastern spiritual tradition, they often discover a deep response within themselves, as though from the depths of their own spiritual yearning. Actually, they experience a desire to be drawn, like the beloved disciple John, into the heart of Christ. John's spontaneous communion with Jesus had little to do with ideas or formulas or rituals.

Often associated with this desire of the Western Christian for intimate union with God is a restlessness and frustration in spiritual life. The person asks, sometimes openly, but often inwardly, "Why does the witness to the Gospel offered by zealous Christians in word, in deed, in writing, even in prayer, so often seem ineffective?" If the questioner is honest, he or she may dare to conclude that witness is not always offered to God alone, only to God, simply to God himself. The Christian may even ask this crucial and sometimes shocking question: "How many really and truly believe today that the *Spirit alone* reveals the Son and draws women and men to the Father?"[3] Is it not true that prayer may sometimes be a subtle means of self-expression rather than a complete surrender to God in the depths of our hearts? Prayer is truly profound when we offer all men and women and the whole of creation to God alone.

We Christians today, perhaps more than ever before, are becoming consciously aware that God is beyond all that we know, beyond all attempts to define him in thought or word, and most especially beyond all our activities that seek to reach him. Today we feel the need for the inner silence of God. The fullness of the sacrament that the Church actually is develops only in profound interiority. Indeed, the authentic quest for God in the West is proved paradoxically by the increasing pain of the seeming absence of God. Western men and women yearn for God's presence precisely because they are often unaware that he is always silently present to them, whether they know it or not. Often our seeming inability to pray is our failure to realize that, in truth, we ourselves do not and cannot pray. Only the Spirit prays within us. The Spirit speaks for us and through us. But when we do not experience communion with the Spirit within us, we sometimes feel that *God* is absent rather than that *we* are simply not present to God.

The call of the Spirit, moreover, is heard with greater difficulty because of the nature of Western culture today. Yet, paradoxically, when God's call is heard, its urgency is greater. Many Westerners cannot resist exteriority, gregariousness, and activism. But intense activity often clouds our human sense of the sacred. We are thus in danger of losing our sense of identity, which is witness to God beyond all forms and definitions. While we live in a society engrossed in a cycle of production and consumption, it is more crucial than ever for us to be in touch with the indwelling God of our hearts. We need holy men and women to remind us of who we are. We need prophets capable of inward silence and peace in order to safeguard our right to be ourselves, to be children of God aware of the Spirit within us, capable of serving one another precisely because of this awareness.

In this spiritual sense, the West has need of the gift which the East can offer. Indian spirituality, for example, offers a challenge to certain more or less accepted Western approaches to prayer. Without in any way betraying his faith, the Christian can deepen his contemplation of divine mysteries through Hindu ways of prayer. From such prayer experience, a renewal of Christian faith may emerge for individuals, and even for communities.

We are speaking here of Eastern ways of prayer, to be sure, not of faith. Jesus Christ was not revealed to the Easterner in India who developed spiritual paths to God over thousands of years without ever having been promised a Redeemer. Therefore, the ancient Hindu searched for his inner "self," the "ground of his being," through an amazing interior experience in which he identified his interior "atman" with the Divine. This experience points, quite indirectly, to the indwelling of the Holy Spirit revealed by Jesus centuries later. Hindu religious experience cannot teach the Christian the revelation given to us only by Jesus. But the Hindu can teach a way of interiority in prayer given to the East by God through cosmic revelation long ago as a gift to all women and men.

Like it or not, the Church is faced with the fact of Eastern spiritual experience and its appeal to countless Western Christians. Whatever we Christians find that is true, good, and beautiful can and should be integrated with our spiritual experience. Nothing admirable in human experience is beyond the reach of the Spirit. The Church recognizes that other paths to God exist of which many Christians know little or nothing. The Indian Hindu world has responded to the inward mystery at the root of the experience of Reality differently from the cultural and religious world of the Mediterranean. The Hindu has always expressed worship chiefly through the search for experience of the Divine at the center of one's being. This Eastern response to God sometimes throws pitiless light on Western attempts to *conceptualize* the Divine, to respond to God with ideas rather than with union in love.[4]

Today the people of God do not wish to repeat the mistakes of Christ's Jewish contemporaries who were unwilling to accept any refashioning of the Mosaic religion. The Church of Christ which recognized Israel's call cannot overlook the preparations for Christ experienced by other religions, even when they present themselves somewhat mysteriously and belatedly to Christians in our day. The cosmic religion given to India by God long before the birth of Jesus can teach us even today the centrality of the search for the Spirit within our own hearts. In the economy of salvation, many paths to God can lead to the everlasting Christ who existed from the beginning.

Christ is not the monopoly of Christians.[5] He is not *only* Jesus of Nazareth. He embodies the divine grace which can lead all of us to God. No matter what form faith may take, there is no way to God except through him. This Christ was already present in Hinduism six thousand years ago. The Spirit of Christ was present in Hindu prayer. Thus the Western Christian who today is somehow drawn to Eastern forms of prayer finds Christ already there. If the Spirit leads us to interior union with God through Eastern ways of prayer, perhaps we shall experience a foretaste of that union of all men and women in Christ which will be fulfilled in the parousia.

At one time within the Church, many Christians felt that contemplation or God experience was a mysterious gift of grace given only to a few rare souls. But Christians today, through their hunger for God, are revealing that communion with the Spirit in the depths of the heart is a gift of God not only to a "spiritual elite" but to all women and men whom God has redeemed. Every Christian—indeed every human being— is capable of experiencing a constant and permanent way of union with the Spirit in the center of his or her being. This way has been expressed through a variety of symbols: the path, the door, the mountain or the ocean. Whatever the symbol, it expresses the call we each receive to communion with God in the Spirit. The Spirit himself speaks to our spirit, whether in the sacrament of the Eucharist or in the desert of silence.

2. Why Eastern Ways of Prayer Attract the West

When a Hindu in India speaks of religion with a Christian, he normally has little interest in doctrine and theology. He seeks no definition of God nor description of divine attributes. Theoretical discussion of the Absolute tends to bore him. The questions that fascinate him are: Have you experienced God? Can you lead me to God? The most profound response of his soul rejects words and seeks only union with God. Abstract reasoning concerning the Divine as well as the Western tendency to search for God outside the self is foreign to him.[6]

The Indian *dharma*, or right way of life, seeks for Reality in the depths of one's own being. To be sure, all holy men and women throughout history, Christian and non-Christian, have sought God within their own hearts. Interiority has always dominated the lives of mystics, whether Eastern or Western. But emphasis on the Divine within men and women has been traditionally characteristic of the Hindu, whether the person be a *sannyasi* (holy one) or not. An interior response to God dominates the spirituality not only of the Hindu monk but often also of the simple villager who leads an apparently "ordinary" life. Interiority is indeed the unique orientation of the Hindu spirit. In both prayer and interpersonal relationships, the Indian responds to the intuitive and experiential rather than to the logical and intellectual. For example, one does not ordinarily become a friend of an Indian through exchange of intimate revelations, but through intuitive presence. Similarly, the Indian experiences the Divine as present to him everywhere and always, not just during worship in the Hindu temple or during certain religious festivals of the year.

Because of this quality of universality in the Hindu experience of God, Eastern interiority appeals today to Westerners who have somehow isolated their prayer life from their ordinary, everyday experience. All men and women respond affirmatively to a sense of unity within their lives. One of the common criticisms of Western Christians is to call them "Sunday worshipers" who establish a polarity between their prayer life and their personal and professional lives. They are said to project the mystery of God *outside* themselves rather than to integrate it within their whole being and total experience. For the Hindu, on the other hand, God is always near. The rickshaw driver in Madras, India, does not hesitate to stop his small auto at sundown to offer his *puja* (worship) to the god Siva while his customer sits quietly awaiting the continuation of the journey. Perhaps some of us Christians today have lost the divine enthusiasm of the first Christians in their experience of the mighty outpouring of the Spirit through Christ. As time has passed, Christian rites and formulas have sometimes assumed an absolute value, a man-made sacredness, which clouds the radiant mystery of Jesus, who rejected soulless ritualism. Christians today often feel the need to reassert genuine spirituality within themselves as opposed to a facade of ritual patterns.[7]

Because the Hindu integrated his prayer with his entire life, he developed holistic methods of asceticism which united his body, mind, and spirit. For the Indian, the total human being prays. Because of his desire to experience God rather than to reason about God, the Indian invented techniques of concentration to lead him to contemplation of the Divine. These methods he called yoga. The Indian *sannyasi* invites others to penetrate to the center of their souls as he does. Thus the Hindu *guru*, or teacher, is essential in the development of Indian spirituality, which cannot be learned only through words. Because men and women need direction in the development of their contemplation of God, the *guru* is believed to be crucial to their spiritual lives. By a kind of osmosis, the Hindu learns how to pray from his *sannyasi*, who already knows how to pray.

Presence of the holy person, more than theological discussion, leads to the Hindu's experience of divine Reality.

It is possible, then, to sum up some of the differences between the approaches to prayer of the Hindu and those of the Western Christian in their present historical developments. In the East, prayer emphasizes being rather than doing; in the West, prayer is too often spoken of in terms of action. The Hindu seeks the Divine in the depths of self, while the Westerner often thinks of God as "in the heavens above." In other words, the Eastern emphasis is on Reality within, or immanence; the Western, on God without or above oneself, or transcendence. In psychological terms, the Western Christian often projects the mystery of God above and beyond the self, while the Indian more often integrates it with his sense of the sacred within the self, and within everyday experience.

If the Hindu speaks of God, the approach is that of synthesis: the person speaks from actual experience, not from intellectual analysis of a preconceived definition. Discussion of spiritual experience relies on intuition, accompanied by little rational thought. Again, unlike the Westerner, the Hindu does not particularly desire to speak of God at all. When a person does speak of God, he or she tends to rely on symbols and analogies without resort to ideas. For example, "Lead me from darkness to light" is more meaningful to a Hindu than any attempt at a rational definition of God, which is regarded as impossible. Because of these Hindu approaches to spiritual reality which have a profound appeal for many Westerners, the methods of yogic prayer have found their way in recent years into the analyses of Western existential psychologists. Thus the Christian of Europe or America who is weary of the inadequacy of rational approaches to Reality is now exploring the spirituality of the Hindu who seeks God not in the mind nor in the heavens, but in the *guha*, "the cave of the heart." For in the center of one's heart is the Holy Spirit sent by Christ who is the only way to the Father.

Many Christians in India today speak of a "new vision" of prayer among Indian Christians formerly trained in Western ways of Christianity "imported" from Europe.[8] This new vision emphasizes the search for cosmic harmony, the idea that the destiny of women and men is linked inseparably with the destiny of the total universe: all creation is divine, the spirit of the universe and the indwelling Spirit in woman and man are one. Accompanying this search for cosmic harmony is the demand for a just and free society for all women and men who share in the divinity of Christ. Here we discover a fascinating continuity between the cosmic covenant and Christian emphasis on the spiritual and corporal works of mercy. In the unique experience of Christ, all spiritual experiences are transfigured. Thus in an era which emphasizes social service, peace and justice for all human beings is linked inevitably with contemplation as the heritage of all women and men in Christ.

The cosmic covenant is actually the law inscribed in the human heart by the very act of creation. The Hindu *dharma* is one of the loftiest expressions of this covenant in all history. When the cosmic covenant is incorporated with Christian tradition as it often is in India today, it escapes both the destructive logic of the Marxist and the disillusioned skepticism of the Graeco-Roman world. This vision reasserts the spiritual against modern counterfeits of the sacred. Jesus Christ rejected empty rites; in fact, he liberated man from every law except love of God and neighbor.

This difference between the real and the counterfeit in the spiritual life is illustrated by a lovely tale of Indian folklore. Once upon a time a lion cub whose parents had been killed by hunters was reared with a flock of sheep. He learned to bleat and to eat grass, and never suspected that he was not a lamb.

One day a lion fell upon the flock. Seeing the lion cub, he asked him what he was doing among the sheep and why he was not ashamed of bleating and eating grass. The astonished cub answered, "Am I not a lamb?" Then the lion took him to a pool of water and told him to look at their two faces reflected in it and to compare them. The lion demanded, "Are you not the same as I am? Is it not your nature to roar? Come, roar as I do." The cub roared, and as he roared he recognized himself and knew that he was a lion.

It is interesting to note that Christians in India today compare the awakening to the cosmic in religious experience discussed above with the great awakening of Hindu witness at the turning point in Indian history in the age of the Upanishads. And some Western Christians compare the incorporation of the cosmic covenant into the Christian tradition with the awakening of the early Christians at the Council of Jerusalem to spiritual values outside those of their own community. These two insights suggest an enriched spirituality on both the vertical and the horizontal levels of contemporary Christianity.

To be sure, many Christians today are not embedded in dogma, ritual, and legalities. But all Western Christians can value the enlightenment offered by emphasis on interior contemplation as opposed to excessive activity in both prayer and ministry. Communion with God in the Spirit is beyond all rites, creeds, and institutions, to say nothing of activism. At the same time, personal union with God cannot be separated from our search for peace and justice for our sisters and brothers in Christ. The second commandment is like the first: those who seek beyond empty rituals love and serve one another as sisters and brothers.

Christians are becoming more aware that the Holy Spirit offers them authentic spiritual experience in communion with all men and women of faith. Thus we recognize the call of the East through the tradition of prayer. This encounter between

East and West can take place only in the Holy Spirit, where all prayer meets and all who pray enter into communion. Westerners who are attracted by the interiority of Eastern prayer have already discovered this truth intuitively. We can identify our own most profound prayer experience with the Hindu insight that we are truly ourselves at a deeper level than that on which we rationalize and philosophize. We realize that to experience the Holy Spirit, we must ultimately allow ourselves to be drawn into the heart of Christ, into the "cave of the heart."

Indeed, the Indian *sannyasi*, like the Western mystic John of the Cross, for example, invites us to penetrate the deepest centers of our souls. There we share in the life of the Trinity, for the center of the soul is the dwelling place of the Spirit. When we experience God within us, moreover, we have a gift to offer to the Hindu. For we are aware of *communion* with the Spirit as the Hindu is not. Even when the Christian experiences the profound grace of mystical union, the person is aware of always retaining his or her own incommunicable individuality. Our response to God is always an I-Thou relationship: "I give myself to you." The Hindu, on the other hand, sometimes negates his own individuality (like the Buddhist) in the total embrace of the Divine because he has not yet found the Holy Spirit. Paradoxically, the Hindu thus helps the Christian to understand the absolute claim of the Spirit upon us in baptism. The Easterner helps us to experience the "todo nada" of St. John of the Cross and the words of Christ to St. Catherine of Siena: "The creature is not." Unlike some Hindus and most Buddhists, the Christian knows that communion is not identity. At the same time, we can learn from the East that union with God always demands a permanent and deepening interiority of Spirit.

The Christian and the Hindu, then, represent today the possibility of a spiritual dialogue which will unite the two strongest ideals of good men and women everywhere: personal union with God in the interiority of each person, and the active search for love, peace, and justice for all of God's children. Christian saints tell us that the person who does not love and serve his or her brothers and sisters in need becomes like a bright, sharp knife which has become rusty from disuse, or like clear water from the fountain which has grown muddy and foul (St. Clement of Alexandria). On the other hand, Christians who teach by words and actions alone, without interior union with the Spirit of Christ in their hearts, are like comedians who act a role upon the stage but possess nothing of what they represent (St. Basil and St. John Chrysostom). By a beautiful historical development in our world, the East is teaching the active Western Christian that service of brothers and sisters is void and empty without union with the Spirit in the prayer of the heart. Through Eastern ways of prayer, we can learn to balance our interior life with the active life of service so long characteristic of us as Western Christians.

3. Comparisons and Contrasts in Eastern and Western Spirituality

In the West, innumerable books are published on the practice and meaning of prayer, meditation, contemplation, mysticism, and faith. Paradoxically, Easterners write of their inward experience of God, while Westerners attempt to explain in rational terms the Eastern experience of the Divine.

Prayer

Eastern prayer is a path of interiority pursued through various ways. Whatever the method of prayer, the Easterner always seeks identity with the source of being, hoping to attain liberation. The Western Christian, on the other hand, is conscious of the self as a person. Through the search for communion with God, the individual person seeks perfection. For the Christian, prayer is encounter between the finite, personal human being and the infinite, personal God. Communion with God is thus a fulfillment of personal individuality. Both Easterner and Westerner seek God in various degrees of freedom, but human fulfillment is stressed by the Christian.[9]

As we Western Christians seek to pray, attention to holy thoughts sometimes leads us to rest in words and their meaning. We may forget that there is no spiritual word or thought which should not pass into love, which should not go straight to the heart, the center of our being where the Spirit lives. The mission of words is communication. They are signs which should disappear into what they convey. When a holy person speaks, for example, not the words pronounced by the mouth and heard by the ear, but rather the inner spirit of the speaker passes through the ear and the mind of the listener to the center of his spirit, the core of his being. In the East, this center of interiority has been called "God's rest," where alone human beings find spiritual peace.

To live a life of prayer is to live in the actual presence of God within our hearts. To do so should be as natural to Christians as to breathe the air around us. To be aware of God's presence, "to pray always" in St. Paul's words, is the definition of a Christian. Thus there can be no part-time Christians.

We Western Christians sometimes become detoured on our way to awareness of God because we get entangled in images and thoughts as well as words. We form mental pictures or ideas about God, and then occupy our imaginations or minds with these images and concepts. Praiseworthy as these exercises are, ideas of God are not God himself: they are simply *what we think about God*. When we attempt to identify the products of our imaginations or intellects with the Reality which is God, they can become idols—just as surely idols as those of metal or stone. God is as near to us as the air we breathe. When we are simply aware of his nearness, we are praying. We cannot pray of ourselves, but we pray without ceasing when we allow Jesus to live in us his life as Son of God. We pray, moreover, when we are aware of God not only within ourselves but within every man and woman and the whole of creation.[10]

Prayer is, then, a universal call to the presence of God. It is a universal theophany or manifestation of God's presence in creation which we experience within ourselves and then within all men and women. Because God lives in all creation, we are responsible for our sisters and brothers who are indeed one with ourselves in Christ. In today's world, we are called to the silence of awareness within a desert of modern noise, and to the love and service of others within a desert of human need. It is the birthright of all of us to lose ourselves within this double mystery.[11]

Speaking one day to an American, the famous Hindu scholar, T.M.P. Mahadevan, asked the Westerner, "Why do you Christians love one another?" The American answered, "We love one another because we are followers of Christ, who commanded us to love one another." Then Mahadevan declared, "That is your problem! You love one another because you are told to do so. We love one another because we *are* one another. All creation is one." This response, while somewhat unfair, points the finger at the Christian who tends "to do what he is told," to center upon the law rather than the Spirit.

Again, we Western Christians sometimes concentrate almost exclusively on the humanity of Christ in our prayer. When we do so, Easterners regard our prayer as anthropomorphic. We sometimes forget that we live always in the loving current of the movement of the Trinity: Father, Son, and

Spirit. Indeed, the Spirit lives in us whether we will or not, whether we are aware of God's presence or not. No darkness can hide us from his glory. To respond to Reality, to pray, is to be aware of the Spirit always present to us, whether in darkness or in light. The presence of God in light and the "absence" of God in darkness are one and the same. Our awareness of both manifestations of the Divine is prayer, communion with God in love.

Because we are all one in God, corporate or common prayer and worship—as well as prayer within the silence of the heart—is our fundamental duty as Christians. Common public prayer is a visible sign of the communion of saints. Just as silent prayer is a witness to the aloneness of God in relation to all creation, corporate prayer unites human beings to one another and to God in worship. Prayer in common is in no sense in opposition to personal prayer. Indeed, we do not distinguish fundamentally between community prayer and private prayer. Rather, we stress the original unity of prayer life within the active participation of all.

We live in a world of communion and interrelationship with our brothers and sisters. It is therefore natural for Christians to read Scripture and spiritual books in common, to meditate in silence on God's word, and finally to share the fruits of such reading and meditation, putting questions to the Spirit and to one another while speaking in all simplicity of what we have read. Thus we offer one another food for silent union with God.

We share the word of God not only in silent gatherings, but more commonly in public when the word is proclaimed during divine worship. But liturgical prayer—official corporate worship—is shallow if it is not grounded in silent contemplative prayer. Liturgical or para-liturgical texts should not reflect a legal mentality of the past but should incorporate our highest values as human beings. Our common texts should as-

similate the richness of interior prayer rather than merely repeat social or political ideas, however good these may be. The
more spontaneous liturgical prayer is, the greater is the need
for inner experience of God as its root. New forms of liturgical
prayer should stress the inner mystery of God's presence and
lead the faithful to taste and long for personal experience of
God as well as peace and justice for all men and women. As
corporate worship, liturgical prayer should call to mind that
our life is one of inward communion with God as well as love
of our fellow men and women. Meditative chants that speak of
this mystery can be drawn from the cosmic covenant as well
as from Scripture. The faithful should go on their way, after
such worship, with silent awareness of the Spirit in their
hearts.

Just as Christians unite with one another in corporate
prayer, they should pray in common with non-Christians.[12]
The great Indian patriot, Vinoba Bhave, used to remark that
Christians can work with Hindus in all fields *except* prayer!
Communion of all women and men is a law of growth; isolation
is a law of death. Thus it is the duty of Christians to promote
unity in prayer with all their sisters and brothers and to seek
universal reconciliation. The call of Christ is not only to proclaim the Gospel but to seek, together with men and women
of other faiths, a return to God, the source of all being.

Joint prayer gatherings and celebrations of religious feasts
can unite people of East and West in mutual enrichment as pilgrims. The famous Ramakrishna monks of India celebrate the
feast of Christmas with Christians as a festival of darkness leading to light. Here, as always, the experience of personal interior union with God among those who pray together is crucial.
Christian and non-Christian come together to share the inner
mystery. In their awareness of the Divine, they enter together
into the universal theophany.

Meditation

Meditation, for many Western Christians, has been regarded as a form of "mental prayer" in which one considers God in his love and all his attributes, or the lives of Jesus and the saints, with the goal of determining the Christian's response to the call of God. The term "meditation" in India, on the other hand, refers to *dhyana*, or contemplation.

In the Indian sense, the meditation of the Western Christian is thus a preparation for pure prayer rather than prayer itself. It is a powerful intellectual exercise, seeking to develop practical convictions which influence the will to do good. But to the Eastern mind, it is an exercise about God, not union with the Divine. Thus the Indian would regard this Western type of meditation as a praiseworthy practice one might follow on the way to contemplation. For the soul ultimately desires God himself, the living God hidden within all creation whom holy women and men come to know in their hearts.[13]

Those who have been trained in Western forms of meditation sometimes acknowledge that their prayer life has developed into a type of emotional prayer made up of fervent aspirations, conversations with Christ present to their imagination, and acts of surrender to God. In such an approach to the Divine, words, images, and feelings offer beautiful consolation to the spirit. To picture the Christ Child in the arms of Mary or to ponder the sufferings of the man Christ on the cross centuries ago is a powerful incentive to Christian living. But why do we sometimes feel a sense of incompletion in such prayer? Is it not because we desire interior union with the living God present within our hearts here and now? The human being was not created to remain within the outer courts of the Holy. Christ on the cross broke down all barriers to the Father. The resurrection opens the heart of man not just to words about Christ, nor images of Christ, nor thoughts about Christ, but to intimate communion with the Spirit of Christ in loving union with the Father.

We might express similar thoughts about the prayers of petition which develop naturally from the traditional methods of meditation in the West. To pour out our souls to the Father in the simple expression of our human needs is a beautiful response to the words of Jesus, "Ask and you shall receive, that your joy may be full." Prayer of petition is humble acknowledgement of our complete dependence upon God. It is an avowal of our nothingness before our Creator.

But again, is it not true that sometimes our prayers of petition develop from a conversation with ourselves rather than with God, that we appear to be informing God of what he knows better than we do? Prayer of petition is interior prayer only when it is complete surrender in union with the anticipated response of the Father. We trust the Father totally; we believe that only the Spirit can act in us and for us. Thus our prayer of petition is inevitably the prayer of the Spirit: intercession in love for all humanity and all creation. We are one with all. Such prayer can save us from the dangerous self-reliance of the Pharisee. If we are truly one with God, the Spirit speaks in the silence of our souls even before we can speak our petition. Ultimately, the only prayer possible is the appeal of the Son to the Father revealed in the Spirit to the man or woman who is one with Christ.

Thus consideration of traditional Western methods of meditation leads us once again to the contrast between the traditional thinking, willing, and doing of many Western Christians and the Eastern way of simply being in the presence of the Divine. To be sure, the mystics of the Western Church, despite cultural differences in the development of their spiritual life, were able to silence "the barking dogs" of talking and doing, and to arrive at interior silence in prayer. St. Teresa of

Avila and St. John of the Cross suffered through spiritual directors who restrained their response to the Spirit in the center of their hearts. In the Western Church we also claim the great mystics of the Middle Ages—Ruysbroeck, Tauler, Eckhart, Marguerite of Porete, and the author of *The Cloud of Unknowing*—the origin of whose spirituality we trace to the desert fathers. These holy men and women felt themselves to be united not so much to a Divinity in "the heavens above" but to the Holy Spirit living within them. Christ was their guide to interior fulfillment. The "interior castle" or the "seventh mansion" where the living God embraces the women and men he has created in love exists always in silence.

The meditation of the Hindu, like that of the Christian mystic, seeks loving awareness of Reality. Therefore yoga, the Hindu spiritual method for striving toward union with God, aims at silencing distractions in order to discover the deep interior self. A word of warning is necessary here. True yoga has nothing to do with a certain false and sometimes vulgarized "yoga" of the West, sometimes expressed in intense exercises and physical gymnastics. Even more important, true *yoga* has nothing to do with a search for the Quietism of seventeenth century Europe condemned by the Church. Neither the liberty of Eastern *Moksha* nor Christian contemplation is found through annihilation of the will and passive absorption. The methods of posture and breath control developed by the Hindu to promote the inward silence necessary for union with the Divine simply prepare the person who practices them for the decisive experience of *samadhi*, a name for the gift of authentic contemplation. While the guidance of a competent *guru* is necessary for the student of yoga, many Indian spiritual teachers lead their disciples daily in meditation, never even suggesting that their followers undertake yogic discipline. Each person, they believe, must find his or her own *sadhana*, or path to interior union with God.

A type of Christian yoga under the instruction of Christian spiritual directors is developing today as a guide to the prayer of inner silence. Men and women of prayer are thus offering a counter-response to the intense activity and distraction of mind with which the Western person seeking true ways of prayer often struggles. These spiritual leaders have discovered an authentic Christian yoga which is effective in growth in prayer within our Western desert of noise.

In no way does incompatibility exist between Christian assimilation of authentic Eastern methods of yoga and Christian emphasis on the history of salvation manifest in the events of the life of Israel within the Old and New Testaments. The key to the Hindu Scriptures, the *Vedas* and the *Upanishads*, is the mystery of the presence of God found in humanity and in all of creation. For the Hindu, this presence is always with us, here and now, whether man is aware of it or not. The Christ who was present in the universe and in humanity from the beginning is the presence sought in Eastern ways of prayer, even though the Hindu is not yet aware of the everlasting Christ. The cosmic presence of God is essential to Hindu meditation. Christians who sometimes pay scant attention to the divine glory within the universe can grow in spirituality through the rediscovery of this cosmic presence.

It is fascinating to observe that Eastern forms of meditation, including Zen, are arousing strong interest in the West precisely at a time when technological progress is at its height.[14] Psychologists and psychiatrists describe contemporary "meditation" as a technique to recover something of ourselves that we have lost in the activism of a technological world. Our human potential to be close to our own selves and to reality has become blurred with time. Therefore we seek methods to rediscover our true selves in silence. In this context, the bridge between psychology and the Christian search for union with God today is obvious: recovering something of ourselves that we have lost is simply recovering our experiential communion with God.

Since the goal of Hindu meditation is eventually to leave behind images and thoughts of God in order to experience the Divine in direct awareness, it appeals to the Western Christian who seeks what he or she somehow knows to be a loss. Hindu Scriptures, combined with the testimony of Indian holy women and men, are the source of Hindu knowledge about God. But intellectual knowledge is not the interior union the Hindu seeks. The Christian who adopts Hindu methods of meditation therefore seeks not just the knowledge of God or of personal emptiness, but communion with the Holy Spirit in the fullness of being. This goal is an I-Thou relationship which can be fulfilled only in Christ.

The East, like the West, has always acknowledged that contemplative awareness of God is a gift. "What hast thou that thou hast not received?" The Eastern *sannyasi*, as well as the Western mystic, understands the implications of divine choice. So do all serious believing people. Mortimer Adler, famous Great Books scholar, once acknowledged that he believes the doctrines of the Christian faith. Asked why he had not joined the Church, he replied, "I do not have the gift of faith." Similarly, a famous Hindu scholar in Madras recently lamented that, despite years of meditation, he had not achieved *samadhi*. Yet all serious believers, Eastern or Western, prepare themselves for the gift of divine union, each through his or her own yoga. A good God eventually responds to those who seek him with their whole heart.

Contemplation

Perhaps the central point of meeting between Eastern and Western spirituality today lies in the significance of contemplation. Back in the thirteenth century, Thomas Aquinas wrote that contemplation is "a simple gaze on the truth." A definition of contemplation written in the 1980's is: "the transcendence of one's own separate personality by the discovery of the one Person who dwells in the heart in whom alone each one of us finds fulfillment." Perfect contemplation, moreover, "is attained through the struggle to achieve the total integration of the human personality in all its dimensions."

The above definition is that of Dom Bede Griffiths, a British Benedictine who has lived in an ashram in south India for more than twenty-five years, and who is acquainted intimately with Eastern approaches to contemplation.[15] The French monk Abhishiktananda (Dom Henri Le Saux), who also experienced Indian spirituality for more than a quarter of a century, wrote: "The real place of divine encounter is the very centre of our being, the place from which all that we are is constantly welling up." This center, symbolized by the heart, is the meeting place of the divine and the human, where experience of God may be granted to women and men. The two great spiritual traditions of Christian West and Hindu India thus meet in the *guha*, the mystery of the "cave of the heart."

In the above definitions of contemplation, we note the Western insistence on God as infinite Person and on the integration of the human personality in all its dimensions. The Hindu emphasis on the absolute necessity of interior union, on the other hand, is beautifully complementary to the Western Christian emphasis on the humanity of the person.

Contemplation, then, does not refer specifically to a life in which many hours of the day are devoted to thinking about God, nor to a life of vocal prayers and liturgical celebrations, however good and praiseworthy these may be. Contemplation means awareness of God at the center of our lives: in him we live and move and have our being. Without even consciously thinking of this mystery, the true contemplative lives continually in a spiritual atmosphere of awareness of God.[16] Christian life is thus directed always toward love of God and love and service of neighbor. We must emphasize that contemplation does *not* mean rare charisma or extraordinary intervention of God. Indeed, the highest spiritual life is the birthright of all Christians. According to Vatican II, "all the faithful of Christ . . . are called to the fullness of Christian life and the perfection of charity."

Because of the emphasis on action rather than contemplation in the Western world today, the encounter of the Church with the contemplative spirit of Eastern religions has been called "the most formidable challenge to the Church in her history."[17] This challenge is to an awakening of deep spiritual growth in the people of God. In response, the Church must stand on her own experience of the Spirit. She must prove her spiritual depth in both contemplation and action. We sometimes hear the cynical remark that Eastern tradition lacks concern for the world, that the Christian vocation today is to build up the suffering earthly city. Such a response must come to terms with the witness of Christ, who offered us the perfect example of interior communion with the Father combined with continual loving concern for his brothers and sisters. The incentive to service of others is universally present to contemplatives. Since to them all is holy, nothing is profane. Fruitful action is a law of being. Not action, but the egoism and personal motives with which we act are opposed to union with God. Pragmatism, under the guise of pastoral zeal, for example, is antithetical to contemplation.

Within Christianity, it may be noted that in our Western youth culture today two principal directions are evident: the contemplative and the political.[18] The contemplative highlights the significance of the influence of Eastern spirituality upon the West. It clarifies the Eastern spiritual dimension of existence over against the political and functionally determined dimension of the West. Significantly, these seemingly opposed elements in East and West are a reality within all of us. They are symbols of two poles within each human being which can create a profound psychological tension. The active Western Christian is discovering today, not without intense pain, the other half of the self which he or she has neglected: the contemplative dimension.

Certain temperaments, moreover, are disposed to a solitary contemplative life, others to a more active life. The world has need of solitaries to remind us that God is an absolute unchangeable Being, that only God *is*, apart from all his manifestations in creation. On the other hand, the world needs men and women to testify to the loving action of God in the people he has created. Solitary contemplatives testify silently to God's presence; active contemplatives are called to build the city of men on the foundation of interior communion with the Spirit.

Thomas Merton expressed well this necessary relationship of contemplation to a world of action:

> What is the relation of [contemplation] to action? Simply this: he who attempts to act . . . for others or for the world without deepening his own self-understanding, freedom, integrity, and capacity to love, will not have anything to give to others. He will communicate to them nothing but the contagion of his own obsessions, his aggressiveness, his ego-centered ambition. . . .

The development of contemplation within the center of our being is actually a release of the power of the Spirit. The touch of the Spirit within us may be at first fleeting, a brief flash of light in darkness. We must be willing to rest in the silence of the Spirit before we can experience the pervasive radiance of light which leads to multiple actions in service to our brothers and sisters—actions which are indeed more of the Spirit than of ourselves. We do not actually possess light; light possesses us.

To be sure, our experiences of daily life often offer sad contradictions to the expectations just described. Too many of us are willing to accept as normal situations which are not merely average but abnormal in a spiritual sense. Christ acknowledged the lack of faith among his followers. The Spirit is given to us in our hearts for communion with others: if we do not share our gift, we do not receive the gifts of others. The offering of self or the refusal of self determines whether or not the Spirit may act in us. Sharing our love is an act of free choice by which we become a channel of the Spirit who directs the whole universe to its ultimate end.

We experience contemplation, uniting our communion with God and loving service, when God chooses to reveal himself to others through us. Every great religious tradition teaches this mystery. Because the Spirit has offered the gift of contemplation to human beings in all ages, each great religious tradition—of East, West, North, South—can learn from each of the others a unique and beautiful manifestation of a particular glory of God. At the present point in history, the East offers to the West its special gift of interior union with the Divine as complementary to the love and service of fellow men and women so characteristic of the Western Christian.

The truly holy person is aware of the deep self that awakens to the inward experience of God at the touch of the Spirit. God plays no favorites. The Father spoke to Western Christians through the prophets of old and through his Son, Jesus. But he never told Israelites or Christians of his cosmic revelations to their Eastern sisters and brothers. Instead, he allows his Eastern children to speak for themselves to his Western children today.

Mysticism

The friends of God have told us in all ages that the ultimate mystery of mystical union cannot be conceived or named. All words one might use are merely symbols that point toward this mystery beyond words or thought. Western mystics have sometimes struggled with a complicated vocabulary to express an experience so powerful that it challenges the language of traditional Christianity. Because these holy people were locked within ritualistic and doctrinal forms of speech, they suffered because of their efforts to speak the truth. Master Eckhart was condemned, Margaret Porete was burned at the stake, John of the Cross was held in suspicion. Mystical experience is a gift of grace not attained by either knowledge of Scripture or intellectual pursuit. Christian experience and Eastern wisdom are one in their testimony to this truth.

Descriptions of mystical experience have been only more or less successful in acquainting the person who has not known the experience with its essence. Thomas Merton used terms which are perhaps more meaningful to the modern Western Christian than statements which have come out of other centuries:

> A mystic is one who surrenders to a power of love that is greater than human and advances toward God in a darkness that goes beyond the light of reason and human conceptual knowledge.

The Hindu mystic, who does not share the Western emphasis on a conceptual approach to reality, would be mystified at the necessity for rational terms in Merton's statement. The Easterner would respond more fully to the mystical poetry of John of the Cross:

Upon that lucky night
In secrecy, inscrutable to sight,
I went without discerning
And with no other light
Save that which in my heart was burning.

It led me through
More certain than the light of noonday clear
To where One waited near
Whose presence well I knew,
There where no other presence might appear.

St. Gregory of Nyssa reminds us that those whom God favors with mystical communion often live in darkness when the light vanishes: the closer a human being approaches to the vision of God, the more that person is aware of the invisibility of God which is darkness. But to the mystic this darkness itself offers more joy than all created light.

The Eastern *sannyasi* warns the Western Christian today of the danger of confusing the joyful inner communion of the mystic with feeling, however admirable. The mystical dimension of human experience goes far beyond loving emotion as well as reason. In institutional religion, this mysterious oneness of God and man is sometimes lost. The human person is created for communion: we come to know the fullness of being only when we realize the Divine present within us. Then the words, "We are created in the image of God," are no longer mere words to us. We actually know ourselves as the likeness of Christ.

Profound mystical experience, unassociated with the revelation of God to Israel and the incarnation of Christ, is found in all great Eastern spirituality, whether it be Hindu, Buddhist, or Taoist. This mystical experience has found expression not only in the *Upanishads* and the *Bhagavadgita;* it has been voiced by uneducated worshipers in Hindu temples and by spiritual followers of authentic Yoga. It also provides an Eastern response to the age-old question of duality or non-duality of God and man in mystical union: the non-dualist Hindu mystic often refuses to say that God and man in mystical union are one *or* two, since the mystery of being transcends all number and all thought.

There is an important difference, however, between the Hindu and the Christian experience of mystical union. For the Christian, Jesus himself is the source of mysticism, and we know that for Jesus, God is a different "I" from his own "I." With God, Jesus has continuous union and communion. His expression of this profound mystery is: "I come from God . . . I proceed from God . . . I am going to God." In the mystery of Christ, the Trinitarian movement from Father to Son and back to the Father in the continuous love of the Spirit encloses the secret of mystical experience.

Whether the mystic is Christian or not, the person who experiences God knows who he or she is. An old Eastern tale expresses this truth beautifully: "Awake, O man and woman, and realize simply that you *are*. You are neither the butterfly dreaming that it is the king, nor the king dreaming that he is the butterfly. *You are yourself.*"

Despite the difference between Hindu and Christian concepts of communion and union, the mystery of the unknown Christ of Hinduism, the Christ who existed from the beginning, is astonishingly present in incipient form in Hindu Scriptures. For example, one reads in *Isa Upanishad 5:*

> He moves, yet he moves not;
> Far he is, yet near.
> He is within all that is,
> And he is outside of all this.

And again, in *Kena Upanishad 2:*

If you believe that you know it well,
As yet you know but little. . . .
He by whom it is thought of, knows it not.
It is not understood by those who understand;
Understood it is by those who understand it not. . . .

The hidden God whom the Hindu has always sought within the center of his being is beyond comprehension. The Christian mystic experiences this God as the indwelling Presence leading us to the bosom of the Father.

Both Christian and Hindu have learned through the testimony of saints that it is possible to enjoy the direct and immediate presence of God in the soul here and now. At least, it is possible to enjoy "a certain degree of this experience," since the full vision of God requires that the body be completely transfigured by the Spirit.[19] But, in union with the Divine even here on earth, St. Bernard tells us, the soul assumes "another form, another glory, another power."

Bede Griffiths points out, once again, that in speaking of communion with the Divine, the Christian will never say, as some Hindu and Buddhist mystics have declared, that the soul in mystic union becomes one in essence with the Divine. Communion is not identity. The Christian mystic does not use the analogy of sparks flying from fire, or the drop of water mingling with the ocean. The person speaks rather of iron heated by the fire so that it is wholly penetrated by fire, transformed by fire, but does not become fire. Indeed, the Christian retains self-identity even in the most profound communion with God possible.

In the Gospel, Jesus offered no teaching to his disciples concerning mystical union, not even to the beloved disciple. He simply commanded his followers to love God and one another. Only God can bring about mystical union with himself. Ultimately, the only evidence the Christian has for the truth

of what he experiences in faith is the experience of Jesus himself. "But there is something else: the testimony of the Spirit
within the mystery of Christ."

Faith

In any discussion of Eastern spirituality for Western
Christians, subjects related to prayer, meditation, contemplation, and mysticism cannot be considered without special ref-
erence to the basic beliefs of Christianity and of the great
Eastern religions. We as Christians readily acknowledge that
we cannot pray, meditate, or contemplate without the gift of
faith in Christ through the Holy Spirit. In fact, we know that
we cannot pray at all unless the Spirit prays within us.
Through cosmic revelation and the testimony of holy men and
women, the Hindu also acknowledges that direct realization of
the Divine is a gift.

But the Christian mystery of faith is of a different order
from the direct realization of being that essentially constitutes
the experience of the Hindu holy person.[20] The certainty of
faith of the Christian transcends the rational, and so does the
sannyasi's realization of being. But Christian faith has to do with
"what cannot be seen" (Heb 11:27), as revealed by the Father
through his Son, Jesus.

In Christian history, however, rationalism and legalism
have tended at times to lessen the sense of the mystery of faith.
In India, on the other hand, the sense of the mystery of being
has always been strong. As a result, millions of Hindus in India
today freely accept as true mysteries of other faiths, including
Christianity. Devotion to Mary, the Mother of God, for example, is common throughout India. On the feast days of
Mary, hundreds of Hindus converge upon Catholic churches
to honor the Mother of God. When special devotions to Mary

take place, young Hindu women are seen placing garlands upon her statue and kneeling before her in prayer. When questioned, they reveal a clearer understanding of the place of Mary in the economy of salvation than some Christians do. "She is the Mother of Jesus," they will declare, "and she answers our prayers."

In short, the basic meeting point of Christian and Hindu lies more in the mystery of belief than in profound theological discussion. The Hindu recognizes that when human beings attempt to seize God in words and concepts, they embrace an idol. We as Christians know that Christ gave spirit and life. The disciples understood the deeper meaning of the words of Jesus only after the Spirit came to them. On the deeper spiritual level, the Hindus—like the disciples of Christ—are aware that they begin to know God only when they realize that they know little about the Divine rationally:

> It is through an awakening that he is found . . .
> As when the lightning flashes . . . the eye blinks, Ah!
> *Kena Upanishad*, 2, 1–4: 4, 4

Reason discusses; experience knows. Theologies direct us to the knowing that will save us. Our minds ponder, but our spirits are completely at home only in awareness of the Spirit at the center of our being. For this reason, the basic task of theology is to prepare us for experience of God beyond all images and concepts.

A fundamental attitude of soul through which the Spirit reveals to man's spirit the mystery of God is demanded by faith. Non-believers sometimes confuse manifestations of mystical union with parapsychic phenomena. But "secondary" manifestations of union with God have always been considered merely incidental by holy men and women. Thomas Aquinas called communion with God stripped of all forms "the experience of wisdom." The great mystics of all ages—men and women like Teresa of Avila, John of the Cross, Marie of the Incarnation, Eckhart, Tauler, and Ruysbroeck—have all testified to faith as the fundamental basis of experience of God: the ultimate mystery of God is at once hidden and made known in the deepest heart of man and woman. On this level, the spiritual experience of the great Western mystics is akin to that of Eastern holy men and women who discover the deepest self through interiority.

The experience of God in faith, present at the heart of the Church, is often latent in the West. In fact, Vatican II made a courageous admission that Christianity seems to have lost all too often its original awareness of mystery. While the Church has never lacked saints, some of us Christians seem to live at a superficial level of awareness of the mystery of faith, content with ritualism and legalism. Moreover, Christian teachers remain too often at the level of morality and emotional piety. Authentic prophets and contemplatives can never reduce their experience of God to images, emotions, and concepts. Interior union with the Divine, combined with love and service of their brothers and sisters, is their goal. The French Christian mystic of India, Abhishiktananda, reminds us that, while Greek thinkers could never perceive a God not identical with reason, "God laughed at Greek reason." He presented himself for adoration as "a helpless object of mockery, hanging on a gibbet." The Supreme "ungraspable, unthinkable, unnameable" God made himself known to man as Jesus Christ. The unmanifest God revealed by the man Jesus is the central paradox of Christianity. Only faith finds a solution to this seeming contradiction.

The Hindu, who responds spontaneously to mystery and paradox, easily accepts the mystery of experience of the Divine. In this context, Christians must accept the fact that profound religious experience—even mystical experience—exists outside Christianity. We must confront the seeming problem of religious pluralism among men and women. We must recognize that the freedom inherent in being aware of the Divine is open to all men and women through the gift of God.

Christian life itself is a life of faith from beginning to end. Both Scripture and the saints of all ages have testified to this truth. The Spirit dwells within us. "Faith is the coming face to face of man with God, the awareness of the divine Presence."[21] Faith, like prayer, cannot be a part-time preoccupation for us. Indeed, faith, prayer, and contemplation are internal realities underlying all that we do as followers of Jesus. They are an acknowledgement of the presence of the Spirit in all persons, and in all creation, always and everywhere. This mystery lies within the Christ who existed from the beginning.

The contemplative dimension of faith is the source through which the Church today must solve the problems of both her own children and a world which cries out for universal faith. Christ has revealed that being is communion. The agonizing thirst for union with all men and women in the Spirit is more evident than ever before in history in both its positive and its negative aspects. The cry of humanity for peace and justice, even when distorted violently, is a cry of the Spirit. The only answer to this agony is unity or oneness in spirit of all human beings. Faithful Christians have testified in every age that God actually interferes in their lives to direct them toward fulfillment in him and in their brothers and sisters. No matter how dark the moment of history, it cannot conceal the glory of the Spirit in oneness with all human beings.

Scripture tells us that God is a consuming fire. The Spirit desires our faith and will not let us rest in our own solitude. Indian tradition tells us, similarly, that when human beings even glimpse the possibility of union with the Divine, they are never the same again. Signs are not enough: we must plunge into the flame. When profound Christian faith encounters deep

Hindu religious experience, the limitations of words and ideas are transcended. Though Western Christians may speak of "higher and higher heavens" and Hindus of deeper and deeper "caves of the heart," the two symbols are complementary. The one transcendent and immanent God does not contradict himself. Yet we Western Christians have profound need to plunge deeper within ourselves to discover in faith the Spirit who desires to act within us:

> The very light which shines beyond all things, beyond the universe, above which there is nothing higher, is the light which shines in the heart of man *(Chandogya Upanishad 3, 13, 7)*.

The Western Church can benefit from the spiritual discipline of Indian tradition to achieve quietness of mind as a prelude to prayer. Freedom from outward distraction in the practice of the concentration required by yogic methods, for example, can open many Christians to the living force of the Spirit. The one Spirit of God in all great religions may lead the Church to explore deeper dimensions of the Gospel, to realize that the Church has still much to learn of the everlasting Christ within the Trinitarian mystery. The "great silence" of the Hindu in his experience of the Divine is complementary to the somewhat common Christian experience of emphasizing Christian life with other persons in the world rather than personal life with the inward Spirit. The silence of soul in which the Easterner encounters his God may be frightening to some active Christians at first. Jesus gave no "methods" of prayer to his followers. But the double command of love of God and neighbor always demands inward as well as outward communion. The only way is the way of love.

As Father, Son, and Spirit are related to one another in the movement of the Trinity, so all of us are related to one another through the Spirit of God. Without union in the Spirit, the only relationship of persons of diverse spiritual traditions is silence, not inward silence, but the silence of lack of communication. We Christians know that silence of being speaks only in Christ the Word. Apart from Christ, this silence remains unbroken. Christ actually lives in communion with all men and women of faith, whether Christian or not. It might be well for us Christians to be aware of the charges of anthropomorphism directed against us by many Easterners. A growing awareness of the Absolute God of all would provide a link of understanding between Christians and millions of Easterners who do not yet know Jesus Christ. Only at the depth of spiritual interiority can the Church solve this problem of faith. The mystery of "the unknown Christ" of Hinduism can open to Christians a possibility of loving union with millions of their brothers and sisters whose faith centers in the cosmic covenant. The mystery of Christ is beyond all our knowledge of him. Faith is the key to a more and more universal response to this mystery.

NOTES

1. Bede Griffiths, "The Sources of Indian Spirituality," *Indian Spirituality in Action*, Bombay, Asian Trading Corporation, 1973, Introduction and pp. 63–67.

2. Abhishiktananda, *Saccidananda*, Delhi, I.S.P.C.K., 1974, pp. 29–30.

3. Abhishiktananda, *Prayer*, Delhi, I.S.P.C.K., 1975, p. 43.

4. Abhishiktananda, *Hindu-Christian Meeting Point*, Delhi, I.S.P.C.K., 1976, pp. 5, 115.

5. Raimundo Panikkar, *The Unknown Christ of Hinduism*, New York, Orbis Books, 1980, pp. 31–61.

6. Vandana, "Indian Spirituality," *Indian Spirituality in Action*, pp. 15–23.

7. Abhishiktananda, *The Further Shore*, Delhi, I.S.P.C.K., 1975, pp. 68–69.

8. D.S. Amalorpavadass, "Prayer Within the New World Vision," *Praying Seminar*, Bangalore, I.S.P.C.K., n.d., pp. 13–47.

9. Anthony Coelho, "Psychology and Prayer," *Praying Seminar*, p. 134.

10. Abhishiktananda, *Prayer*, pp. 1–31, 52–56.

11. Joseph Neuner, "The Universal Call to Contemplation," *Praying Seminar*, pp. 112–114.

12. Albert Nambiamparambil, "Praying with Members of Other Religious Traditions," *Praying Seminar*, pp. 199–205.

13. Abhishiktananda, *Towards the Renewal of the Indian Church*, Ernakulam, India, K.C.M. Press, 1970, pp. 29–36.

14. John B. Chethimattam, "Meditation: A Discriminating Realization," *Journal of Dharma*, April 1977, pp. 164–72.

15. Bede Griffiths, "Mystical Theology in the Indian Tradition," *Jeevadhara*, October 1979, pp. 275–76.

16. Abhishiktananda, *Prayer*, p. 60.

17. Abhishiktananda, *Towards the Renewal of the Indian Church*, p. 10.

18. C. Satyananda Tholens, "Hindu-Christian Dialogue," *Interfaith Dialogue in Tiruchirapalli*, eds. X. Irudayaraj and L. Sundaram, Madras, Siga, 1978, pp. 119–22.

19. Bede Griffiths, "Moksha in Christianity," *Interfaith Dialogue in Tiruchirapalli*, pp. 15–18.

20. Abhishiktananda, *Saccidananda*, pp. 198–99.

21. Abhishiktananda, *Prayer*, p. 12.

SUGGESTED READINGS

Besnard, Albert-Marie. "The Influence of Asiatic Methods of Meditation," in Christian Duquoc and Claude Geffré, eds., *The Prayer Life*. New York: Herder and Herder, 1972.

de Foucauld, Charles. *Meditations of a Hermit*. New York: Orbis Books, 1981.

de Mello, Anthony. *The Song of the Bird*. Garden City, New York: Image Books, 1984.

Faricy, Robert. *Seeking Jesus in Contemplation and Discernment*. Wilmington, Delaware: Michael Glazier, Inc., 1983.

Geffré, Claude and Gustavo Guttierez, eds. *The Mystical and Political Dimensions of the Christian Faith*. New York: Herder and Herder, 1974.

Griffiths, Bede. "Mystical Theology in the Indian Tradition," *Jeevdhara*, IX (1979), 262–77.

Johnston, William. *Christian Mysticism Today*. New York: Harper and Row, 1984.

Johnston, William. *The Inner Eye of Love*. New York: Harper and Row, 1978.

Lossky, Vladimir. *The Mystical Theology of the Eastern Church*. Crestwood, New York: St. Vladimir's Seminary Press, 1976.

Maloney, George. *Manna in the Desert*. New York: Living Flame Press, 1984.

Nomura, Yushi. *Desert Wisdom*. Garden City, New York: Doubleday, 1982.

Panikkar, Raimundo. "Faith—A Constitutive Dimension of Man," *Journal of Ecumenical Studies*, VIII (1971), pp. 223 +.

Pennington, Basil. *Challenges in Prayer*. Wilmington, Delaware: Michael Glazier, Inc., 1982.

Zaehner, R.C. *Hindu and Muslim Mysticism*. London: Athlone Press, 1960.

Love, Service, Wisdom:
The Three Margas

Indian spiritual leaders have spoken traditionally of the three *margas*, or ways to achieve *moksha*, or liberation. They are: love *(bhakti)*, action or service *(karma)*, and contemplative wisdom *(jnana)*. None of the three is practiced in its pure form. Gurus seek to integrate them, with particular emphasis on one or the other according to a person's belief, inclination, temperament, and spiritual development. All can be combined with yoga, which is physical-mental discipline through posture, breath control, and concentration directed toward the achievement of the peace and quiet desirable for meditation and contemplation. The Hindu does not stress corporate salvation as we do. Each person must work out his or her spiritual liberation. Mutual encouragement is practiced, however, and the guru is reverenced as a guide in whatever path to God the

44

individual chooses to emphasize. The name *raja marga* is some-times used to describe the unification of all *margas*.

Path of Love: Bhakti Marga

Bhakti is union with God here and now through prayer, love, and devotion.[1] This experience is expressed in a personal, dynamic relationship. Faith and surrender to God are essential. The God of the *bhakti* is believed to be deeply concerned about human beings. His divine interventions in human forms, or *avatars*, re-establish the rule of truth and justice, or *dharma*, in the world. Among the greatest *avatars* are the gods Rama and Krishna. They inspire human beings to relate themselves personally to the God who desires love and union with men and women. Total attachment to God in love is the *bhakti* ideal.

In the classic *Bhagavadgita*, the god Krishna speaks in *bhakti* terms to the hero Arjuna:

> When a person offers to me with devotion only a leaf, or a flower, or a fruit, or even a little water, this I accept from that yearning soul because it is offered with love from a pure heart.
>
> Whatever you do, or eat, or give, or offer in adoration, let it be an offering to me; and whatever you suffer, suffer it for me.

A famous example of *bhakti* prayer appears in the writing of the Hindu philosopher and holy man, Sankara. He speaks to a loving God in complete surrender:

> Whatever I speak is my prayer to you; all my art is my symbol of worship of you; all my movements are toward

you in veneration; my food is an offering of oblation to you; my lying down is prostration before you; all my joys are in dedication to you. May whatever I do be a synonym of my worship of you!

This prayer of Sankara exemplifies perfectly the total self-gift of union with God in love which is the path of *bhakti*. The worshiper can express love in many ways. According to Hindu tradition, there are eleven *bhakti* approaches, all really one in nature, to complete surrender to the God of love. Among these are union with God as lover, as child, as servant, or as worshiper living in continual interior adoration of the Divine. The last approach is evidently that of a contemplative.

The Hindu *Bhagavatam* also speaks of seven ways of *bhakti* devotion practiced by the faithful: listening to God, serving him, obeying him, praising him, sacrificing to him, adoring him, and consecrating oneself to him completely. All of these paths to God are different ways to seek union with the Divine in the center of one's heart. The Hindu feels free to emphasize one or more of these paths in the direction of his or her whole life.

Indians express their creativity in seeking their own paths to adoration of God. Image worship, for example, is acceptable in *bhakti marga*. The sacred image is in no sense an idol, just as the innumerable Hindu gods do not contradict the one Absolute God. The image is simply a center of concentration where God is believed to be present in a special way, and where one can perform a ritual of *puja*, or worship, in a highly symbolic form. *Bhakti* also freely encompasses music, dance, sculpture, and architecture as integral elements of worship. The Hindu desires to involve his whole being in his love of God. The poet Rabindranath Tagore expresses this attitude of worship beautifully:

I believe that the vision of Paradise is to be seen in the sun-
light and the green of the earth, in the beauty of the human
face and the wealth of human life, even in objects that are
seemingly insignificant and unprepossessing. Everywhere
in this earth the spirit of Paradise is awake and sending
forth its voice. It reaches our inner ear without our knowing it. It tunes our harp of life which sends our aspiration
in music beyond the finite, not only in prayers and hope,
but also in temples which are flames of fire in stone, in pictures which are dreams made everlasting, in the dance
which is ecstatic meditation in the still centre of movement.[2]

It would be easy for the Western Christian of today, bom-
barded daily with the violence of the world and the threat of
nuclear destruction of the planet, to read the above with a
somewhat jaundiced eye, but saints and artists see more than
the rest of us. And the *bhakti* is close to the infinite God revel-
ing in the joy of the world.

Christian Bhakti Marga: Path of Love

We Christians can indeed enrich our prayer and worship
through the ways of *bhakti*. Christianity itself has been sometimes called a *bhakti marga* in India since it centers in love and
worship of God incarnated in Jesus Christ. Though Jesus is not
an *avatar*, and the Hindu knows that Jesus is a *unique* incarnation of God, he sees an analogy between the Christian's love
for Jesus and his own love for a chosen *avatar*, whether it be
Krishna or Siva. The desire of the Hindu is to call upon all
creation to help him to develop awareness of the God who is
always aware of his creatures.

Bhakti offers us Western Christians full interpretations of many types of interpersonal relationships with God in prayer and with our brothers and sisters in love and service. The beauty of the *bhakti* path may be valuable to many of us who tend to reject certain types of music, dance, and symbolic rites in prayer. We sometimes separate ways of worship from the life of worship, rather than concentrating on our basic interior attitudes in prayer. Thus we often are uneasy in using beautiful art objects or symbolic gestures in worship. We accept sacramental rituals such as the Eucharist because they are divinely instituted by Christ. But we are often intolerant of beautiful rituals that are entirely symbolic.

Paradoxically, some of us tend to hold on to traditional rites and formulas that have somehow lost their significance in Christian practice. At the same time, we fail to realize the essential place of symbols as self-expression in creative prayer and worship. How many of us feel free, like the Hindu, to choose our own private symbolic forms of worship according to our own inclinations, capabilities, and circumstances? Our inward relationship with Christ can develop profoundly through the expression of our love in symbolic forms. *Bhakti* encourages us to choose our own way of personal prayer, not to imitate in routine repetition the prayer of persons who lived perhaps centuries ago. When we choose a personal symbolic reminder of the presence of God in our own private prayer, it is difficult for us to fall into a false recital of prayer formulas unrelated to our inner life. An Easterner who receives a personal *mantra* or prayer from the guru, for example, accepts it gratefully as a dynamic call to a unique union with the living God. It expresses a mysterious relationship with God that he or she sometimes shares with none. It calls the person to immediate experience of the Divine within the self.

Bhakti worship also emphasizes group prayer. Characteristic of such prayer is a union of participants in spirit that makes us one in our experience of love and worship. Mere bodily presence to one another is not enough. In Christian India, for example, the divine sound-symbol *OM* is often the very center of group sound-prayer called the *bhajan*. To participate in the *bhajan* is to feel the presence of the Spirit in the united worship of all present in prayer, song, and music. Christians in India today also chant the symbolic sound *OM* in para-liturgical services. The beauty of the sacred symbol *OM* becomes a dynamic center for united devotion. Group prayer can be meaningless unless it springs forth from communion with the Spirit in the hearts of all those who pray as one. Western Christians can discover, in the *bhakti* spirit, their own sound symbols—old or new—to give life to their group worship of the living God.

The *bhakti* path of love is obviously unlimited in its suggestive power for prayer. It centers in pure devotion as a chosen approach to God without negating the paths of service and contemplation.

Path of Service: Karma Marga

The faithful performances of our duties (called *dharma*), without attachment to the fruits of our good actions, is *karma marga*.[3] The world of action is the realm of *dharma*, according to the Hindu, but action alone cannot lead us to liberation. Thus this path of service rejects artificial distinctions between the sacred and the secular. By performing our daily duties selflessly for God, without desire for reward, we repudiate a dualism of being and doing. We do not renounce joy in our service of others, but we reject egoistic self-satisfaction. Thus our actions have a positive meaning as love for God and for our fellow human beings. According to the *Bhagavadgita*, service to which we are not attached is not binding but freeing:

He whose undertakings are free from anxious desire . . .
whose work is made pure in the fire of wisdom—he is
called wise by those who see.

He is glad with whatever God gives him, and he has
risen beyond the two contraries here below: in success or
in failure he is one: his works bind him not.

Offer all your works to God, throw off selfish bonds,
and do your work. No sin can stain you then even as waters do not stain the leaf of the lotus.

Hindu *karma marga* is in no sense a substitution of action for
interiority: it is a way of life which is crucial to the ultimate
meaning of life in the world of service. If we offer all our actions to God while at the same time seeking success and status,
we are outside the path to God—or at least on its margin.

It is interesting to note that all Hindu masters insist on the
gospel of inner detachment in the world of action. Ramakrishna, a nineteenth century Hindu saint, used the image of
the lotus in teaching his disciples: the lotus rests in muddy water but rises beautifully from the earth. Rama Maharishi declared that to discover the true self which penetrates beyond
all superficial levels of personality, we need not leave the world
of action. We should stay where we are, but pursue self-in-
quiry. Swami Ramas taught that non-attachment is a positive
virtue: the attached person loves only some of his brothers and
sisters, but the spiritually detached person loves everyone. Finally, Mahatma Gandhi pointed out that for the good person
there is no escape from active service of all: the many are manifestations of the One, and the One may be reached through
the many. Universal love, however, can be achieved only
through spiritual asceticism. Then our everyday actions become living prayers. In short, a whole spirituality can be built
around *karma marga*, or good actions, as continual worship of
God in the Spirit.

Christian Karma Marga: Path of Service

Traditionally, good actions in the world have often been given a second place to contemplation in Christian history. Only in our own day, as we reject the dichotomy of the sacred and the secular, as we come to realize vaguely the non-dualism of man, do we begin to appreciate the struggle to achieve the total integration of the human personality in all its dimensions.

What we sometimes do not always appreciate in practice, however, is that *karma* or action alone is not enough. Just as medieval Christians sometimes viewed loving service to one's brothers and sisters as inferior to a cloistered life of prayer, so today we sometimes reject the life of contemplation as inferior to total service of the neighbor. Thus an unacceptable dichotomy is created once again: the old false duality is reinstated. Both views are symbolic expressions of an attitude which is non-holistic.

In the Gospel of Matthew, Jesus rejected this false dichotomy. Gandhi, though a Hindu, wholeheartedly accepted the Sermon on the Mount as a *sadhana* or way of life. The beatitudes are a perfect expression of Jesus' teaching on the Christian life. Each beatitude unites contemplation and action: the blessedness of union with God is one with service of one's brothers and sisters. Those who show mercy receive mercy. The peacemakers are children of God. Happy in spirit are those who suffer for others. Gandhi had learned from the teaching of ancient Hindu *sannyasi* that for men and women of faith there is no duality between union with God in spirit and good actions. Moreover, action without spirit is empty. The ideal *karma marga* is based on communion with God flowering into good works. On the other hand, all Hindus are not Gandhis, and all Christians are not saints. Spiritual emphases differ. Today we Christians can teach many Hindus that, for most human beings, spiritual communion with God is not enough of itself. To love and to serve others is essential. But the contemplative Hindu can often teach us—perhaps with greater power—that action for the neighbor is not enough of itself. Saints, whether Hindu or Christian, have learned over centuries the beautiful reciprocity of contemplation and service through which one places all trust in the Spirit. Of ourselves we can neither pray nor act. The Spirit within our hearts prays and acts through us. From the fullness of our hearts we serve our neighbors. Contemplation and compassionate ministry become one.

Path of Contemplative Wisdom: Jnana Marga

Jnana Marga is the search for that wisdom which leads to enlightenment through faithful reflection and contemplation.[4] The person who follows the way of *jnana* seeks the unchanging Reality living in all things. At the same time, he or she seeks the one eternal Spirit beneath the changing modes of human consciousness. The experience sought through *jnana marga* is essentially mystical, because it is beyond sense and reason in the "ground" or "center" of the soul. This experience of God, known as *saccidananda*, is the inexpressible "ultimate being in pure awareness, resulting in spiritual bliss." Among Hindus, it is the final goal of all religious quest. *Jnana marga* is usually considered to be the highest path to God, just as the mystical way is often seen as a "higher path" in the Christian tradition.

A true *jnani*, however, is one who is entirely available to God and open to his inspiration.[5] A person who refuses to do his share of the world's work on the excuse that he must find peace and quiet for contemplation is in no sense an authentic *jnani*. The contemplative who is really free sees the world within and the world without, solitude and society, silence and conversation, for what they are: not contradictions but reciprocal relationships, like interior prayer and compassionate service. The sense of the universal presence of God, which is at the heart of Indian spirituality, is actually the greatest possible incentive to good works.

The Hindu *jnani*, then, emphasizes contemplative wisdom in his spiritual quest, just as the followers of *bhakti* and *karma* concentrate on devotion and good works. Yet no one of these paths to God excludes the other two.

Christian Jnana Marga: Path of Contemplative Wisdom

According to Christian mystic Bede Griffiths, of Saccidananda Ashram in south India, the experience of God of the ancient Hindu *sannyasis* is no less unique and fundamental for humanity than the experience of their contemporary Hebrew prophets. The wisdom of India is the inheritance of the Indian Christian, just as the wisdom of the Old Testament is the inheritance of the Western European Christian.

A Christian interpretation of *jnana marga*, Dom Bede declares, stresses three important considerations.

First, Indian wisdom recognizes the need to transcend both sense and reason in meditation and to discover the center or depth of the soul where each person may meet God directly. According to *Katha Upanishad 2, 2*:

> He who, by means of meditation . . . recognizes the Ancient, who is difficult to be seen, who has entered into the dark, who is hidden in the cave, who dwells in the abyss, as God, he indeed leaves joy and sorrow far behind.

The experience described is obviously mystical.

Second, the experience sought through *jnana marga* is an experience of grace, or a gift of God. Again, Hindu Scripture states in *Katha Upanishad 2, 23*:

> That Self cannot be attained by instructions or by know-ledge or by much learning. He whom the self chooses, by him the Self can be attained.

The experience described here, writes Bede Griffiths, corresponds with what in Christian tradition we call "contemplation," a knowledge of God beyond sense and reason, communicated by the Holy Spirit. Men and women can prepare for this gift through the path of *jnana marga* or contemplative wisdom, but only God can grant it.

A third consideration is that a Christian interpretation of *jnana marga* will differ from the Hindu concerning the exact relationship between God and the soul in mystical experience. For the Hindu non-dualist, no distinction remains between the soul and the personal God in this experience—rather, both disappear in the one Reality of the "Absolute Brahman." For the Christian, however, the soul discovers its own inner depth or personal being in mystical experience, but at the same time discovers the presence of the Holy Spirit, communicating life and light and love to the soul. For a Christian, experience of God is a communion of love. The Holy Spirit is the very love of God poured into the heart communicating the bliss of union. All feeling of duality vanishes, but the soul and God remain distinct. At the same time, the Christian feels a oneness with all men and women and all creation. The Spirit leads the loved one to "the depths of being which is the Father, the Godhead of all."

While recognizing the gift of the Holy Spirit which comes to us through Christ alone, we Christians can learn much from the ancient wisdom of *jnana marga*, the highest Hindu path to

God. The way of the *jnani* admits of no compromise. The person who follows this path to the end asks and expects nothing for the self. Perhaps this is why certain Western Christians seek God in the solitude of the Himalayas, following the way of the *jnani*. Simplicity is always at the core of sanctity.

Today Western Christians, in their inquiries into ways of spirituality, are discovering through psychological analyses of personality that various methods of prayer are suited to persons of various temperaments. Thousands of years ago, the people of India were aware that different personalities chose different *sadhanas*, or paths to God, and called them *margas*. Indeed contemplation itself and the ways of contemplation are as old as the human heart.

NOTES

1. Michael Amaladoss, "Bhakti Marga," *Praying Seminar*, pp. 155–59, 162–64. See also Noel Sheth, "Towards an Indian Christian Spirituality," *Indian Spirituality in Action*, pp. 118–21.

2. Rabindranath Tagore, *Contemporary Indian Philosophy*, pp. 45–46.

3. Michael Amaladoss, "Karma Marga," *Praying Seminar*, pp. 171–79.

4. Dom Bede Griffiths, "Jnana Marga," *Praying Seminar*, pp. 184–85.

5. Abhishiktananda, *Saccidananda*, pp. 152–59.

SUGGESTED READINGS

Appasamy, A.J. *The Theology of Hindu Bhakti*. Madras: Christian Literature Society, 1970.

Braybrooke, Marcus. *The Undiscovered Christ*. Madras: Christian Literature Society, 1973.

Buhlmann, Walbert. *The Search for God*. Maryknoll, New York: Orbis Books, 1980.

de Mello, Anthony. *Sadhana: A Way to God*. Garden City, New York: Doubleday and Company, 1984.

Klostermaier, Klaus. "Sadhana," *Religion and Society*, XVI (1969), 36–50.

Klostermaier, Klaus. "Sannyasa," *Indian Ecclesiastical Studies*, VII (1968), 8–40.

Neuner, Joseph. "Bhakti and Christian Meditation," *Clergy Monthly Supplement*, III (1956–57), 177–90.

Schnapper, Edith B. *The Inward Odyssey*. London: Allen and Unwin, 1965.

Stevens, Edward. *Oriental Mysticism*. New Jersey: Paulist Press, 1973.

A Road to Contemplation: Yoga

Hindu Yoga

Prayer is a gift of God to all men and women. We learn to pray from those who pray like us and from those who pray differently from us. Human beings are called to find spiritual unity in diversity.

The East, especially India, has always been drawn so strongly to the prayer of silence that it has sought continually for methods to help men and women to enter upon this way of prayer. In general, these methods are termed yoga. The word "yoga" itself is interpreted variously. Broadly, it designates any spiritual path, such as *bhakti-yoga*, *karma-yoga*, or *jnana-yoga*, as already discussed. India's holy men and women have developed these *sadhana*, or spiritual paths, as guides for the inner journey to God. These methods are meant to prevent people from stumbling on the spiritual way, and especially to establish them in the silence and discipline without which interiority is almost impossible.

Traditionally, yoga is a discipline whose aim is to bring the mind to the quiet necessary for interior prayer. The great Hindu Swami Vivekananda once remarked that "consciousness is like a drunken monkey jumping at random from tree to tree." Yoga aims to restore order to the distraction, dissipation, and chaos of undisciplined consciousness.[1]

The beginning of Patanyali's classical treatise on yoga states: "Yoga is a psychological and physical discipline which is an unequaled method of self-mastery. Yet the authentic practice of yoga has as its goal not magnificent feats but the discovery of the innermost center of the soul by way of interior silence."

Today in the Western world much confusion exists as to what yoga really is. Westerners often confuse *hatha-yoga*, a physical discipline alone, with yoga proper. They define yoga as a series of physical exercises that cure disease and produce good health. Others regard yoga negatively as a kind of abstract, godless "mysticism" which leads the soul to empty isolation. Still others see it as the art of attaining superhuman powers. The true yogi, however, has nothing to do with the occult or hypnotic powers. He or she defines yoga as concentrated effort toward the spiritual goal of seeking the Divine. There are different schools of authentic yoga, but all have the same spiritual goal. In the *Bhagavadgita*, Lord Krishna tells his follower, Arjuna:

> When the restlessness of the mind, intellect, and self are stilled through the practice of yoga, the yogi with the help of the Spirit within finds fulfillment and joy beyond reason.

Yoga is thus more than a technique or discipline; it is a path to total commitment of the person to the Spirit.[2]

In the Western popularization of yoga, this real purpose is often lost. Technique is confused with essence. True yoga brings us to that independence in which we are simply ourselves, aware of our own being. Yogic meditation aims at helping us to reduce our field of consciousness to an indivisible point, to master our flow of thought, to guide our spirit to the silence in which we may find God. Yoga leads us to the light in which we abandon ego-expression as useless. The yogic achievement of *samadhi*, or liberation, is the climax of a disciplined journey. Here we discover a new mode of being, the hidden real self. Thomas Merton expressed the true yogic *samadhi* when he wrote that contemplation is not and cannot be a function of the external self. There is an irreducible opposition between the deep self that awakens in contemplation and the superficial, external self. The latter, says Merton, "will disappear as smoke from a chimney." Experience, rather than intellectual analysis, establishes this insight.[3]

Christian Yoga

We can assert, then, that the goal of yoga is the prayer of inner silence. The way of yoga has been found and tried among Christians. The ultimate aim of Christian yoga is contemplation. In the progress of true yoga, there is a movement of ascent to pure consciousness, a realization of the self beyond space and time. For the Christian, says Dom Bede Griffiths, this ascent has already taken place in the resurrection of Christ. Because Christ has redeemed us, we can rest in our own pure state of being even in this life.[4]

Surely we Christians are called to train our faculties in

preparation for the gifts of the Holy Spirit. Wisdom, the highest of these, makes us partakers of the Divine. To receive wisdom, we must prepare ourselves in silent waiting. In other words, the goal of Christian yoga is to lead us to the stillness of self-awareness in preparation for communion with the Holy Spirit.

It should be pointed out here that although we have masterful guides to spiritual advancement in *The Imitation of Christ*, *The Ascent of Mount Carmel*, *The Dark Night of the Soul*, *The Interior Castle*, and other Western spiritual classics, *physical* aids to spiritual discipline are dealt with only sketchily in these works. Therefore, we have ample scope to draw benefit from the experience of yoga.

While it is true that yogic exercises are very helpful in achieving inward silence in prayer, it is also true that yoga is not essential for silent prayer. The Spirit calls each of us as the Spirit chooses. Moreover, as Indian spiritual masters often repeat, yoga is not recommended to all indiscriminately. The calling and the temperament of an individual will indicate whether yogic methods will be helpful or not. If one finds yoga to be personally ineffective, he or she should discontinue its practice. The value of Christian yoga, however, is unquestionable.

Like all spiritual paths, yoga has its own risks. Just as a person needs guidance in any serious spiritual journey, one should not proceed to the later stages of yoga without a sure guide. The spiritual director should be one who has studied Holy Scripture, who has followed the path of yoga without variance between teaching and practice, who has had at least a glimpse of his or her spiritual goal, and who has the prudence and compassion to lead others. The true Christian guru understands the following crucial test: so long as a person continues to think and to feel in prayer, he or she is still outside the spiritual castle. God is beyond. Nothing can satisfy the soul but God himself. Interior silence is true praise of God:

> The silence will be a simple listening to the Spirit within and without, a simple looking at the One who is present within and without, simply being attentive, being aware. . . .

Ultimately, there are no "techniques" in the spiritual life, says French mystic Abhishiktananda (Dom Henri Le Saux), except in the "outer layers" of it. Printed maps and guides exist for the ante-chambers of the spiritual castle, for the external courts. Signs appear on the outside gates. But the last miles of the spiritual path must be walked by each one alone. "Doors will open themselves one after another, from inside, once faith and love are strong enough." Sincere followers of yoga have the following to learn from yogic discipline: it is a proved means to achieve the quiet and silence which make it possible for the Holy Spirit to act freely in the soul. The true yogi has found that essential freedom which places no limits on responsiveness to the Holy Spirit.[5]

J.M. Dechanet, an American Benedictine, in his book, *Christian Yoga*, suggests that total consecration to God demands integration of all the faculties of body and soul. A calmed mind, quiet nerves, and silence clear the path for the highest consciousness of God. In this context, the greatest obstacle to God-realization, says Swami Prabhavananda, is laziness![6] Buddha called procrastination in the struggle to experience God the greatest sin. And Christ himself said: "No man, having put his hand to the plow, and looking back, is fit for the kingdom of God." The path of yoga—or any true path of spiritual discipline—is a challenge to reorient one's fundamental attitude in seeking God alone.

Various Exercises of Yoga

Competent Christian gurus have examined seriously which of the many, many yogic practices directed toward meditation and contemplation may be integrated fruitfully within the Christian life. The spiritual guide who teaches the way of yoga is ordinarily one who believes that intellectual knowledge alone is often inadequate as a way to experience God, one who has already achieved the spiritual goal of the yogic path. This guide has learned through experience that certain yogic exercises—such as physical postures *(asanas)*, regulation of breathing *(pranayama)*, and concentration *(dharana)*—are helpful for many Christians, particularly those who tend toward distraction of mind and dissipation of consciousness. Whatever the method of achieving it, inner silence is necessary for the Christian who desires to go beyond the prayer of the beginner in the spiritual life. Following are yogic practices proved to be of value to Christians.

The Eight-Fold Path of Yoga

For thousands of years Hindus have sought God through the eight-fold path of yoga which is directed toward experience of and union with Reality. Through interior continuity, this path moves gradually through a deeper and deeper spiritual experience from the lower layers of consciousness to ultimate union with the Divine. Following are descriptions of the classic eight paths. The first two are more or less preliminary to yogic experience, since they elaborate on the right conduct necessary for the beginner in the spiritual life. In the following six paths, this chapter will propose practices for the Christian who wishes to engage in yogic experience, normally under spiritual direction. Pursued faithfully, these practices can lead to calm interior integration and ultimate contemplation.

1. First Path: Moral Preparations

The first path, called *yama*, recommends five basic "abstractions" necessary for the beginner in the spiritual life.

Non-Violence is a term made famous by Mahatma Gandhi. As true yogi, we cultivate a positive desire to heal and to conserve life. We resist anger, hatred, and revenge. We are ready to forgive with an open heart.

Truthfulness is practiced in thought, speech and action. We seek to know the truth sincerely and to live it with honesty and simplicity.

Sexual Continence is the practice of a continence proper to our state in life. The yogi believes that sexual continence in thought, word, and action increases our moral stamina and mental vigor.

Non-Stealing refers not only to our avoidance of the evil of taking what belongs to another, but also to the forms of stealing witnessed in both capitalist and socialist societies in which the motives of power and profit often deny human dignity and the rights of labor.

Non-Greed means keeping our desire for status and wealth in check by living honestly and justly.

2. Second Path: Religious Observances

The second path, called *niyama*, also deals with moral disciplines which the yogi considers fundamental for a beginner in the search for God.

Purification calls for cleanliness of mind and body in the person who desires to follow the spiritual path of yoga.

Contentment is an attitude of peace and even joy in all our experiences as a preparation for the gift of contemplation. Contentment is especially necessary in hardship and suffering that we cannot remedy.

Discipline means that we accept the daily problems and vexations of a good life. It is not necessary to seek austerities for their own sake.

Study of the Self is a preliminary to the practice of concentration necessary for contemplation. Knowledge of one's temperament, for example, may suggest that spirituality should center in one of the three *margas:* devotion, service, or wisdom.

Worship of God means that we must surrender ourselves to the Lord and accept our own personal limitations in our search for enlightenment.

3. Third Path: Physical Postures: Asana

The two paths just described are regarded in the East as so obviously necessary to the spiritual life that they are often barely mentioned. The third path, called *asana,* therefore begins the real practice of yoga. The word *asana* itself refers to various forms of physical posture. It includes all those aspects of health, hygiene, and posture which keep the body fit and relaxed and the mind prepared for the concentration necessary for meditation. The movements of the *asanas* are derived from the beautiful movements of living creatures in nature: balance, gliding, flexibility, swiftness, circling, and stillness. The vitality and strength of these postures center in the attitudes with which we perform them. For example, to simply sit in a firm, erect position, with the spinal column held free, will bring vitality to prayer if we do so with quiet concentration.

Lord Krishna, in the *Bhagavadgita*, expresses the beauty of the *asana* in his words to his follower, Arjuna:

> Let the yogi find a place that is purified and a seat that is restful, neither too high nor too low. There let him practice yoga for the cleansing of his soul, with the life of his body and mind in peace, his soul in silence before the One. With upright body, head, and neck, which rest still and move not; with inner gaze which is not restless but still. . . . With soul in peace and all fear gone, and strong in the vow of holiness, let him rest with his mind in harmony, his soul concentrated on me, his God supreme. The yogi who, lord of his mind, always prays in this harmony of soul attains peace . . . the peace supreme that is in me. . . . Yoga is a harmony. . . .

Major Practices of the Third Path: Meditative Postures

The following postures not only soothe and calm the body; they arouse spiritual energy latent in the person.[7] To be sure, there is no magic in these experiences. They simply set into action certain means given to us by God. Grace turns the harmony established to fruitfulness, and we become more balanced and healthy in mind and body, more dynamic, more able to shoulder the responsibilities of a Christian, and more receptive to God.

Calmness of spirit has its counterpart in physical postures. Practiced faithfully, these exercises can help to recondition the muscles and nervous system, as well as stimulate and regulate the whole metabolism.

Presumably no one will be able to run through this series of postures from start to finish at the first attempts, although the exercises are really less striking than they appear to be at first glance. They are only a few of an indeterminate number of postures that may be developed. We should proceed at our own rate of achievement without concern about lack of complete success in accomplishment. Perfection in posture develops slowly just as perfection in meditation does.

Lotus Posture

Sit on the ground in a firm, erect posture, with the spinal column held free. Bend left leg and place foot on right thigh, drawing left ankle inward. Bend right leg and place foot on left thigh in similar fashion. Soles should turn upward, with knees remaining on floor. Place hands over the knees with palms open upward, and the thumb and second finger of each hand touching, forming a letter O.

For thousands of years, the basic Lotus Posture has been assumed in India, not only by yogis but by ordinary people as well. Because of its calming effect, it has become a classical pose for concentration and meditation.

Perfect Posture

Sit on the ground in a firm, erect posture, with the spinal column held free. Place the heel of one foot on top of the heel of the other in such a way that both heels fit comfortably into the angle formed by the parting of the two thighs. Knees should touch the floor. Place hands on knees as in Lotus Posture.

This emotionally relaxing posture has been used by the great saints and yogis because it is conducive to meditation. It remains the easiest and most graceful posture for long periods of prayer.

Auspicious Posture

Sit on the ground in a firm, erect posture, with the spinal column held free. Bend the right knee and place the sole of the right foot against the left thigh. Bend the left knee and push

the toes of the left foot between the right thigh and the calf.
Place hands on knees as in Lotus Posture.

The Auspicious Posture and the Perfect Posture are recommended for persons who find the Lotus Pose too difficult.

Pelvic Stretch Posture

Kneel down, sitting firmly on heels. Turn heels somewhat out with the toes nearly touching, to form a kind of sad-
dle. Stretch backward slowly, with arms pushing straight
down for support. Raise pelvis and hold as long as you are rea-
sonably comfortable. Then come forward, resting buttocks on
heels and head on floor with arms extended forward.

Variations of the Pelvic Pose can be developed. These
postures have a beneficial effect on the nerves and vital organs,
relaxing the body before meditation.

Further Practices: Meditative Postures of Devotion[8]

Prayer Posture

Stand up straight, keep feet close together, close eyes, relax body. Turn the mind inward, breathe consciously, think of the Holy Spirit living within you.

Posture of Devotion to the Master

Stand up straight, open your eyes, imagine you see before you the Risen Lord as your universal Master. Bend forward, touch his feet, receive his blessing. Ask the Lord to open your inner eye, your eye of enlightenment.

Palm Tree Posture

Stand up straight, hold your feet eight inches apart, focus your eyes on one point, relax your body, breathe consciously. Stretch one hand upward. Stretch both hands upward. Now clutch your hands crossed in front of you. Feel a balance and totality before the Lord.

Practices of Third Path for Physical Discipline

In the 1980's, when problems of emotional instability and tensions loom larger in the West, there is a greater emphasis on integration of body and mind. Yoga can be a preventive system, helping to maintain body and mind in normal health. Yogic exercises have been said to provide an "oxygen cocktail" more vivifying than artificial stimulants. Rhythmic bends and twists, for example, increase mobility of arms and legs, lubricate joints, and help to create a supple, flexible spine. Yogis report that gentle, flowing motions synchronized with breathing improve both circulation and coordination.

In all these postures of the Third Path, the spine is to be kept erect, in one straight line with the head, neck, and trunk of the body. We human beings are the only inhabitants of earth who have a vertical spine; in animals the spine extends horizontally. Yoga reminds us of this truth: it is a symbolic link, rising vertically between earth and heaven. When yogis sit with legs crossed, they often visualize a spiritual stream running from the top of their head to the ground, forming an axis around which their body is molded. Body and spirit become one.

The aim of the following postures is to bring calm and peace to our entire being, to make the body a faithful companion of the spirit, to free the spirit from anxieties and problems common to all of us, and finally to arouse the spirit to prayer. The spiritual person understands the need for the discipline inherent in these exercises.

Symbolic Yoga Posture

Sit in either Lotus or Auspicious Posture described above. Hold left wrist with right hand, and right wrist with left hand. Bend left, then front. Bend right, then front. Breathe consciously and rhythmically. Exhale, suspend breath, inhale. Posture improves circulation.

Angle Posture

Stand up straight. Hold feet twenty-four inches apart. Breathe consciously and rhythmically. Hold left hand in mid-chest area, bend head to right, bend body to left. Hold right hand in midchest area, bend head to left, bend body to right. Posture gives flexibility to body, especially the spine.

Forward Bend

Sit on the floor with legs extended before you. Raise arms high over head, stretch spine upward, inhale deeply. Keep back straight. Exhale, lean forward, bringing tips of fingers to touch toes. Do not bend knees. Stretch forward from the pelvis without forcing. Remain as motionless as possible. Posture stimulates entire body.

Cobra Posture

Lie on stomach with palms pressing against floor at shoulder level, fingers forward. Successively raise head, neck, and upper back as high as possible, keeping lower half of body, from navel downward, on floor. Inhale slowly, exhale. This pose may be retained thirty seconds and repeated ten times with even breathing. It provides complete stretching of neck, shoulders, and spine.

Shoulder Stand Posture

Lie flat on back, inhale, raise both legs together slowly until whole body attains as vertical a position as possible, with elbows resting on floor and both hands supporting the back. Press chin against chest, and breathe naturally. Try to hold position without motion. Increase time of posture gradually. Return to relaxed position. Posture strengthens lower back, helps to regulate weight, and refreshes the mind.

Relaxation Posture

Lie on your back, arms along sides with palms up, legs apart, body held loose. Close your eyes and relax body from head to toes, breathing in slowly and deeply. Relaxation should be practiced to assimilate benefits of yoga exercises. Hindus call this posture the Dead Pose; Americans call it the Sponge. It offers revitalizing power and rejuvenates the tissues of the body.

Fourth Path: Breath Control: Pranayama

Fundamentally, *pranayama* consists in various approaches to the inhalation, exhalation, and retention of breath, under the guidance of a qualified teacher.[9] When breath is controlled, the mind is quiet. Rhythmic breathing is a preliminary exercise for calming the mind. Regulation of breathing is of various types. Breathing exercises are simple at first, but a guide is needed to progress in *pranayama* before going on to more advanced exercises in breath control and to the later stages of yoga.

Breathing is the most obvious manifestation of energy or vital force in our bodies. Control of this vital force has many implications. It is often considered to be the source of so-called "faith healings." This is true, according to the great *yogi*, Vivekananda, whether those who practice such healing realize it or not. Energy is omnipresent in the universe, first in the individual body, then beyond it.

Methods of breath control have been practiced for centuries by Zen Buddhists and Taoists as well as Hindus. Lao-tzu asked his followers: "Can you govern your breathing so that it is soft as a child's? Can you govern your spirit so that it never strays away?" In general, Eastern Christians have been aware that practiced breathing gradually becomes calm during prayer, especially during the rhythmic repetition of a sacred prayer formula like the Jesus Prayer. Christian *pranayama* is thus an aid to the quiet and peace necessary for contemplation.

Practices of the Fourth Path: Breath Control

Sectional Breathing[10]

Sit on the ground in a firm, erect posture with your spinal column held free. Place each foot on the opposite thigh. Place both hands on your abdomen. Breathe deeply in and out so that your hands feel the air pouring into and out of the lowest part of your lungs. Shift your hands to your sides and perform the same exercise. Shift your hands to your back and repeat the same exercise.

Variations: Sectional Breathing

Place both hands on your *mid-chest* area, breathe with your *mid-chest*, and perform the above exercise. Shift your hands to your sides and repeat the same exercise. Shift your hands to your back and repeat the same exercise.

Place both hands on your *mid-chest* area, breathe with your *high chest*, and perform the above exercise.

Place both hands on *either side of your hips*, breathe with your *high chest*, and repeat the same exercise.

Place both hands on your *back* at your *high chest* area, and repeat the same exercise.

Complete Breathing

Place your left hand on your abdomen, your right hand on your *mid-chest*. Breathe deeply, filling the abdomen first, then the *mid-chest*, then the *high chest*. Retain the breath for a few seconds, then breathe out, first abdomen, then *mid-chest*, then *high chest*. Inhale, retain breath, exhale. Repeat six times. Complete breathing should be practiced in the morning or evening before taking food, in a quiet well-ventilated room. It should be followed by spiritual meditation.

Fifth Path: Withdrawal of the Senses: Pratyahara

In this fifth of the eight-fold paths, the powers of the senses become one with the powers of the mind. The mind becomes calm and controlled, and the centers of the brain do not form objects perceived by the senses. *Pratyahara* is not a part of the early stages of yoga because one cannot control the mind until one knows experientially what it is capable of doing. This stage of yoga has been compared with "the return of sun rays to the sun at sunset": the rays seem to become one with the circle of light of the sun. Similarly, the senses withdraw and become one with the light of the mind.

The person practicing yoga is therefore ready for this fifth path when the mind is calm and under control. It is no longer attached even to thoughts that have resulted from practicing the earlier stages of yoga. In the *Bhagavadgita*, Lord Krishna calls the individual in this stage of prayer a person of "steady wisdom." Krishna speaks of this experience in symbolic terms: "When the yogi withdraws the senses completely from their objects, as a tortoise draws in its limbs, then wisdom is firmly fixed."[11]

Not much practical advice is given by the Hindu masters as to the practice of this stage of spiritual development. Vivekananda suggests that, at first, the yogi just sit and let the mind run on, while observing the various forms it takes. After a time, thoughts will grow fewer, and eventually the mind will become calm and under perfect control. "Steady wisdom" will be achieved. Western Christian mystics speak of an analogous stage of spiritual development as gradually achieved "detachment" of the soul in seeking interior union with God.

Samyama

The final three stages of the eight-fold path—*dharana*, *dhyana*, and *samadhi*—are often called by the single word, *samyama*. These are the highest stages in mental discipline, meditation, and contemplation. At least in their beginnings, they are difficult of achievement for anyone, whether Hindu or Christian. They have been compared to the two "dark nights" recorded by John of the Cross. In the early stages of *samyama*, a person may experience the purgation called "night

of the senses," caused by unsatisfied craving for worldly plea-
sures. In the later stages, the individual may experience "the
dark night of the soul," an intense suffering of a spiritual nature
endured by those advanced in the mystical life. *Samadhi* itself
is the final stage of mystical union with the Divine in pure
awareness and bliss.

Sixth Path: Dharana

In this sixth path, the mind seeks at first to concentrate on
a particular image, form, or object, bringing the attention back
to it again and again when the mind wanders.[12] This development in the eight-fold path may be compared with what
Teresa of Avila calls "the first degree" of contemplation, in
which the will is fixed on God but the imagination wanders.
Constant practice of concentration is necessary to achieve the
"one-pointedness" of mind which is the goal of this stage of
meditation. Both Hindu and Christian saints record that un-
wanted words and images now intrude upon the field of concentration, making meditation difficult.

Although the Spirit within may be discovered after much
prayer and repeated renunciation of the senses, the saints recognize that the search for interiority is not easy in the stage of
dharana. Therefore, the purified mind may seek help by fixing
the gaze on an image of the Lord. Thus the meditation may
combine exterior image with the silence of interiority. The dis-
turbance of soul found in the sixth path is a preparation for the
joy of final union with God.

The person may experience laziness, doubt, lack of enthusiasm, lethargy, grief, or mental distress. In the *Bhagavadgita*, Lord Krishna advises the yogi to fix the mind on the light
within his or her heart, on the heart of a holy person, on a
happy dream, or on "anything that appeals to one as good."

Moreover, the yogi should seek solitude as much as possible until true contemplation is found in simplicity and patience.

If one compares this sixth path of yoga with the contemplative way of John of the Cross, *dharana* corresponds with "active contemplation" as preparation for "infused contemplation." In this active stage there is a combination of the person's action and God's action. But in Saint John's "infused contemplation," as in the seventh and eighth paths of yoga, the spirit finally surrenders to God every initiative for its spiritual development.

Seventh Path: Dhyana

The seventh stage of the eight-fold path, *dhyana*, is the unbroken flow of the mind toward the Spirit.[13] The person in prayer now discovers the power of letting the mind flow in an uninterrupted current toward the Divine. Distracting forms and images normally disappear from consciousness, and the mind is fixed on the one Spirit within. This direct flow of the mind is compared with Zen in Japan and Ch'an in China. Though the person may still experience a certain strain in self-direction, concentration on the Spirit is achieved. Christian spiritual directors tend to discourage the formation of mental pictures of Christ at this stage, and to recommend simple interior contemplation without images.

The way of *dhyana* is based upon listening, meditation, and contemplation. In order to listen to God speaking to the soul, interior silence is necessary for peace of heart. Control of the senses, exterior and interior, is taken for granted at this stage. The mind seizes the message heard, centers upon it in complete attention, and finally rests in contemplative peace and joy.

Stillness is stressed. The Spirit hidden within the self

must be sought in "the cave of the heart." In Indian terms, the true self is experienced only when "knots of heart," or dominance of the senses, are broken. Then the soul is capable of experiencing union with God in peace. It is ready for the final stage of mystical union.

As in the case of *dharana*, few spiritual directions are given, as the Lord himself will guide the person in this stage of spiritual development. Ordinarily, however, the yogi sits in solitude, withdraws into the self as "a tortoise withdraws its limbs," fixes the mind on the Lord simply, lovingly, and faithfully, and rests in complete attention to the Spirit.

The Eighth Path: Samadhi

Samadhi is the final stage of the eight-fold path, the perfection of *dhyana*. The Spirit is experienced in interior light, and the soul is united with the Divine. It is sometimes called a "super-conscious state" by the Indian. It is also compared with the "unitive way" of Western Christian mystics. Various types of *samadhi*, increasing in subtlety, have been described by *sannyasis*, just as there have been varied descriptions of the unitive way in the spiritual literature of the West. Fundamentally, the experience of *samadhi* as deep interior union with Spirit rejects all that is external to soul.

It is hardly necessary here to refute types of false "samadhi" described by persons seeking "supernormal powers" divorced from the spiritual life. The constant practice of cessation of all mental activity, the repression of all thought in order to make the mind a complete vacuum, is an empty "achievement." Such a practice results only in stupefying inertia. Though certain yogic practices may result in unusual psychic powers, these are not sought by the true yogi, who desires the perfect liberation of union with the Divine. Moreover, *samadhi* has no relationship to passive experiences of persons under the influence of certain drugs. These refutations must be asserted in our day because of a proliferation of fake "ashrams" in which undisciplined persons without spiritual insight seek "overnight mysticism."

The truly spiritual person who experiences *samadhi* may be in an "illuminative" state, a term used by John of the Cross and called a "cloud of virtue" by the Hindu. Lord Krishna, in the *Bhagavadgita*, describes the person who has achieved *samadhi* thus:

> Joy supreme comes to the *yogi* whose passions are at peace, who is pure from sin, who is one with God. . . . He who sees me everywhere and all things in me, to him I am never lost, nor is he lost to me. . . . He who is in this oneness of love, loves me in whatever he sees. He looks on the pleasure and pain of all beings as he looks on them in himself. Wherever this man lives, in truth he lives in me.

Krishna goes on to tell Arjuna that those who are perfect in yoga are "those who have fixed their minds on me, and who, endowed with supreme faith, worship me."

Holy men and women, both Hindu and Christian, humbly remind us that the attainment of contemplation is no guarantee of its permanence. Spiritual discipline is necessary. To focus the mind on the Spirit within one is no easy achievement. Dark, subconscious forces discourage even the sincere. One who has had a glimpse of inner Reality comes to enjoy the vision of the Spirit only through discipline. The voice of conscious discipline is not always heard even by good people.[14]

A comparison of Hindu *samadhi* with the experiences recorded by Christian mystics is valuable for the Christian who seeks God in prayer. In Christian paths to God, the help of images is normally called up to the degree of meditation called "discursive prayer." In later stages, or "the prayer of simplicity," mental images are discarded and a "simple intent" or "naked interior gaze" remains. This stage of prayer, since effort of will is no longer required, is called "acquired contemplation." It can be compared with Hindu *dhyana*, except that in the latter images of God are sometimes retained. The experiences of *samadhi* and of Christian mystical union have often been expressed in similar terms. But Christian mystics have always insisted that mystical union is always an experience of *communion* with God, while Hindus are willing to express union with God as loss of human identity in the Divine. True mystics, Christian and non-Christian, have often reported their experiences in surprisingly similar terms. The differences are sometimes due to cultural variations in expression. The goal of the ultimate experience of the Christian in mystical union (and perhaps of the yogi, too) is best expressed by Christ: "That they all may be one as thou, Father, art in me, and I in thee; that they also may be one in us." In the words of Bede Griffiths, interior union with the Spirit means oneness: "Our destiny is to be one with God in a unity which transcends all distinctions, and yet in which each individual being is found in his integral wholeness."[15]

NOTES

1. Abhishiktananda, *Hindu-Christian Meeting Point*, Delhi, I.S.P.C.K., 1976, pp. 94–222.

2. Benigna Lobo, "Initiation to Yogic Prayer," *Praying Seminar*, Bangalore, I.S.P.C.K., n.d., pp. 262–70.

3. Frank Podgorski, "Sāmkhya-Yoga Meditation: Psycho-Spiritual Transvaluation," *Dharma*, April 1977, pp. 152–63.

4. Bede Griffiths, *Return to the Centre*, London, Fount Paperbacks, 1978, pp. 137–46.

5. Abhishiktananda, *Prayer*, Delhi, I.S.P.C.K., 1975, pp. 44–49.

6. Swami Prabhavananda, *The Sermon on the Mount according to Vedanta*, Sri Ramakrishna Math, Madras, India, 1972, p. 73.

7. J.M. Dechanet, *Christian Yoga*, New York, Harper and Row, 1972, pp. 84–108.

8. Brother Amaladoss and Benigna Lobo, "Yoga Asanas and Pranayama," *Praying Seminar*, pp. 271–72.

9. John Moffitt, *Journey to Gorakhpur: Reflections on Hindu Spirituality*, London, Sheldon Press, 1973, pp. 147–48.

10. Amaladoss and Lobo, *op. cit.*, p. 273.

11. Moffitt, *op. cit.*, pp. 149–50, 151–55.

12. T.K. John, "Initiation to Dhyana," *Praying Seminar*, pp. 274–78.

13. See Moffitt, *op. cit.*, p. 155.

14. Bede Griffiths, *Return to the Centre*, pp. 143–46.

15. *Ibid.*

SUGGESTED READINGS

Amaldas, Swami. *Christian Yogic Meditation*. Wilmington, Delaware: Michael Glazier, Inc., 1983.

Cuttat, J.-A. *Christian Experience and Eastern Spirituality*. Paris: Desclée and de Brouwer, 1967.

Dechanet, J.M. *Christian Yoga*. New York: Harper and Row, 1972.

Eliade, Mircea. *Yoga: Immortality and Freedom*. London: Kegan Paul, 1958.

Matus, Thomas. *Yoga and the Jesus Prayer Tradition*. New Jersey: Paulist Press, 1984.

Neuner, Joseph. "Yoga and Christian Meditation," *Clergy Monthly Supplement*, III (1956–57), 89–101.

IV

A Buddhist Way of Meditation: Vipassana

A well known Buddhist path for seeking union with reality is *Vipassana*, which means insight achieved through concentration in meditation.[1]

Although our discussion centers on Hindu ways of prayer, the relationships between Hinduism and *Vipassana* will be valuable to the reader who will note at once the meeting points of practices of yoga and *Vipassana*.

Vipassana is much more than concentration as such. It is *not*, as some Westerners suspect, a means to solve theories of philosophy or theology. And it is not a means to acquire supernormal powers, nor to escape from the problems of life through self-hypnosis. It is just as opposed to "insight without effort" as Hinduism is opposed to "overnight mysticism." In short, it is a method of meditation, an art of living cultivated through concentration of mind which is a means to true insight. *Vipassana* tells us to look, to observe in a special way. Its goal is to get to the heart of reality, to relate ourselves to all reality in an attitude of love, peace, and joy. As a method of meditation, it helps us to first get in touch with the heart of reality within ourselves. Through constant practice of concentration it can lead to two objectives: purification of mind, and cultivation of a new insight toward reality which arises spontaneously and progressively. *Vipassana* is thus designed to help us to *experience* the passing nature of many realities in our lives.

Buddhist forms of meditation, like Hindu *sadhanas*, had their origin in India. Historically, Buddhism spread throughout the East, Japan, Sri Lanka, Nepal, and other countries, where different Buddhist paths to reality were developed. In India itself, Buddhism was absorbed, more or less, by Hinduism. Therefore it is no surprise that the practices of *Vipassana* suggest many of the guides to meditation found in Hindu yoga. For example, *Vipassana* and yoga both developed eight-fold paths, though these paths differ in many respects.

Vipassana is based on the teaching of Indian mystic, Gautama Buddha, who believed that suffering is inherent in life and that one can liberate oneself from it through mental and moral purification. Buddha taught that the chief cause of suffering is inordinate craving for pleasure, happiness, and life itself. This craving, which is often unconscious, can be destroyed through the eight-fold path of enlightenment. The steps of this path are: right view of life, right personal resolve, right speech, right action, right means of livelihood, right effort, right mindedness, and right concentration. The ideal of Buddha is an asceticism of universal love. If we understand that all living beings are both suffering and impermanent, then it is necessary that we experience reality as changing in ourselves. *Vipassana* attempts to make us intensely aware of the suffering necessary to achieve the Buddhistic ideal.

If *Vipassana* is "a map for living," we may ask ourselves

how it may be helpful to the faithful Christian. Like Hindu
yoga, it may be a complement to preparation for Christian
prayer. No genuine approach to prayer needs to be foreign to
a Christian. We have no quarrel with the Buddhist ideal of an
asceticism of universal love. We cannot accept completely,
however, "the four noble truths" of the Buddha: "suffering exists; suffering has a cause; suffering can be destroyed; there is
a way to destroy suffering." Buddha knew nothing of the suffering of Jesus Christ, our Redeemer. The value of suffering
was unknown to him. Yet he understood through cosmic revelation the goal of universal love among human beings. Christian saints would indeed agree with him that "earthly realities"
are fleeting and that love is the ultimate law of life.

What, then, can *Vipassana* offer us specifically in our
prayer? Buddhism is not prayer in the Christian sense for us
who know that Jesus suffered, died, and rose again. Christ
gave us a new definition of suffering. But as an art of meditation, as a method of experiencing thoughts of love and peace,
Vipassana can be a beautiful preparation for prayer, and thus
participates in prayer. Again, *Vipassana* is not prayer in the
sense of personal communion with God in the total self-gift experienced in true contemplation.

But, ironically, many of us Christians objectivize a personal God and pour out our hearts to him; yet we do not experience the "I-Thou" relationship with God which is true
contemplative communion. Surely a way of prayer in which
one speaks to God as object is undesirable for a Christian.
Some of us, moreover, over-emphasize the external and the legal in our prayer and meditation. Eastern ways of meditation
like *Vipassana*, in their emphases on the interior life, sometimes
lay bare certain selfish motivations in our unconscious of which
we, as "active Christians," are unaware.

For us, the touch of Christ indeed transforms everything.
Thus the love experienced by a faithful Christian through a

Buddhist *method* of meditation is no other than the love of God poured out upon the soul through the Spirit of Christ. The Christian who seeks God in true contemplation may well find *Vipassana* to be a preparation for communion with the Spirit in the depths of his or her being. In the long run, there is often a closer relationship between the revelation of the cosmic covenant and the word of Christ than we realize. It has often been repeated that the Buddhist dives into the ocean of Reality to obtain the pearl of great price. The Buddhist believes the pearl to be the service of love itself. The Christian believes that God is love, and the pearl of great price is the kingdom of God within us where the Holy Spirit lives.

Practice of Vipassana: Buddhist Path of Meditation

The method of preparation for meditation called *Vipassana* has three steps.[2]

The first is *Anapana Sati*, through which we concentrate on inhalation and exhalation of breath. Breathing is common to all living beings independent of race, caste, or religion. Breathing is also intimately connected with our thought processes. In the proposed exercises, concentration on breathing moves from gross to subtler objects, from the physical through the psychological to the spiritual aspect of our thoughts, and finally to communion with our innermost selves.

The second step is *Vipassana* itself, which consists of our concentrating on sensations of the different parts of the body, such as heat, cold, throbbings, and pulsations. When we give our attention to the various parts of our bodies, the reactions formerly produced because of emotionally charged activities are partially reproduced. While we are aware of these reactions in meditation, as more or less neutral observers, the scars of past emotional involvements disappear to a degree (as happens in psychoanalysis at the moment of catharsis through awareness).

The final step is *Metta Bhavana*, or meditation on love, through which we move out of ourselves to embrace all of creation in a spirit of love. Through this exercise we experience purification and inner peace. Thus we can send forth our love even to our enemies in a spirit of complete reconciliation. Of course, our purification must be sincere if we are to offer our gift of love to others in truth. A spiritual guide is necessary as one advances in the practice of *Vipassana*.

1. First Stage: Concentration on Breathing

Sit on a straight-backed chair in a relaxed posture, with your feet firmly on the ground. Hold your back erect and your body fairly immobile.

Direct attention to your breathing at the point where your breath enters and leaves your nostrils.

Keep your attention on your natural, continuous flow of breath, without any deliberate deepening of your breath, and without any attempt to force it into a definite rhythm.

Keep your attention at the point where the air strikes your nostrils. You will have a fringe awareness of the passage of your breath through your body, but do not focus your attention on it.

Your attention should be gentle, relaxed, not forced. When your mind wanders, bring it back gently to the breathing point at your nostrils.

You will notice that a natural calmness gradually descends over your whole body, while your breathing automatically regulates itself. You will also become gradually more and more aware of subtle sensations at your nostrils as your breath enters and leaves. Actually, your mind is becoming sharper and sharper through the process of concentration. It is becoming attuned to subtle reality rather than to coarse sensations.

You will discover that your mental states affect your breathing. When you are angry, for example, your breathing is affected at once. Thus attention to your breathing puts you in touch with your mental state. Breathing is both an intentional and an unintentional action, so that concentration on breathing makes you aware of what is unintentional in yourself.

Once you have achieved concentration on breathing, you are ready for the second stage of *Vipassana*.

2. Second Stage: Concentration on Bodily Sensations

Direct your attention to the crown of your head and be aware of whatever sensations you feel there. Move your attention to the right side, to the left, and then to your whole head, aware of what you feel. Now move your attention to your eyebrows, your eyes, your chin, throat, and the back of your head. Linger on each part, feeling the sensations there. Then move your attention downward to the trunk of your body, your back, your shoulders, arms, hands, thighs, legs, feet, down to your toes. Just concentrate on sensations. The sensations felt may be various: heat, cold, pain. Note each sensation, or no sensation, without preference. If you feel no sensation in a particular part of your body, linger there a little longer, and come back to that part more often. At least, you will be aware of the part of your body to which you direct your attention.

Repeat the process again and again, even for long periods. As you progress, instead of sensing smaller parts of your body, concentrate on integral parts like your head or your entire arm or leg. Sense each part as a whole.

Maintain a sense of composure. Do not be elated when you have pleasant sensations, nor dejected when you feel unpleasant or painful sensations. Equanimity in pleasure and in pain is an important goal of *Vipassana*.

Pain that you have not experienced before will be felt in different parts of your body, partly because you are not accustomed to concentration, and partly because impurities in your being are slowly released through concentration. Now concentrate more and more on those areas where you feel pain, and let the pain move out of your body.

Vipassana is a purifying process: you will experience relief as unhealthy vibrations—anger, hate, jealousy—leave you and healthy vibrations predominate. Part of the purifying process is due to the fact that your mind is concentrated not on the past and the future but on present situations here and now.

With the practice of *Vipassana*, you will gradually develop a new insight into life. A period of time is recommended in which you will meditate on the eight-fold path of the Buddha. After achieving a right view of life and a right personal resolve, you will move on to the next three aspects of the eight-fold path, called *Sheela*, which means right speech, right action, and right occupation. Sinful action in body and in speech must be avoided.

Samadhi, or concentration of mind, refers to the last three aspects of the eight-fold path: right effort, right awareness, and right concentration. Through continual concentration on emotional changes, equanimity is maintained at the very onset of undesirable feelings like anger and hostility. Right thoughts and right attitudes lead to wisdom, which produces a balanced, detached, and peaceful mind.

3. Third Stage: Disinterested Love—Crown of Vipassana

Concentrate on your whole body, from the crown of your head to the tips of your toes, which you perceive as one mass of vibrations, good and bad. In a purifying process, let all the vibrations of anger, hatred, or ill-will leave your body, so that only good, healthy vibrations remain.

Now picture in your imagination all the people around you: your family, friends, community, townspeople. Imagine their unhealthy vibrations as leaving their bodies, so that only their good vibrations remain. Now concentrate on yourself again, feeling vibrations of love, compassion, sympathy for others in their suffering and in their joy. Feel within yourself deep, endless peace. Repeat this meditation many times. You will feel your body charged with good vibrations. You will feel power moving out of you for the benefit of all: the power of love, peace, and joy.

If the practice of *Vipassana* leads us to self-knowledge and to the peace necessary for communion with God, it is a desirable form of preparation for deep personal prayer. Again, the East can teach us how to prepare for our deepest spiritual experience in the Holy Spirit.

NOTES

1. Ishanand Vempeny, "A Buddhist Form of Meditation: Vipassana," *Praying Seminar*, pp. 186–97.

2. Ronald Prabhu, "Initiation to Vipassana," *Praying Seminar*, pp. 310–16.

SUGGESTED READINGS

Geffré, Claude and Mariasusai Dhavamony, eds. *Buddhism and Christianity*. New York: Seabury Press, 1979. (Essays by Frits Vos, Mariasusai Dhavamony, Maha Sthavira Sangharakshita, Dominique Dubarle, Mervyn Fernando, *et al.*)

Graham, Aelred. *Zen Catholicism*. New York: Seabury Press, 1975.

Johnston, William. *Christian Zen*. New York: Harper and Row, 1981.

Johnston, William. "Dialogue with Zen," in Christian Duquoc, ed., *Secularization and Spirituality*. New Jersey: Paulist Press, 1969.

Johnston, William. *The Still Point: Reflections on Zen and Christian Mysticism*. New York: Fordham University Press, 1980.

Merton, Thomas. *Mystics and Zen Masters*. New York: Farrar, Straus, and Giroux, 1967.

Merton, Thomas. *Zen and the Birds of Appetite*. New York: New Directions, 1968.

Ross, Nancy Wilson, ed. *The World of Zen*. New York: Vintage Books, 1960.

V

Scriptural Prayer:
The Bible and the Upanishads

------

1. The Biblical Prayer of Christ

In discussing Eastern ways of prayer for Western Christians, we have noted that Jesus did not offer methods of prayer to his followers. But we learn how to pray by listening to the words of Christ in Scripture and by observing his actions. In Holy Scripture God speaks to women and men. The Bible also describes the human response to the word of God. Yet we find little recorded of the actual prayer of Jesus to his Father in the four Gospels.

Consider, for example, the oldest Gospel, that of Mark.[1] Jesus is presented as a teacher and healer in Galilee, a prophetic voice announcing the coming of God's rule. Mark certainly reminds us that Jesus prayed. He frequented the synagogue and

91

went on pilgrimage to the temple, gave thanks for food, and celebrated the passover with his disciples. Jesus also taught his disciples that they must pray when confronted with the power of evil, and when faced with the terrors of the end time. He condemned the hypocrisy of the scribes for their pretentious "long prayers," and he praised the devotion of poor widows.

As for the private prayer of Jesus, Mark records the event, but seldom the prayer itself. We read that Jesus rose early in the morning, long before dawn, and went off to a lonely place and prayed there. Directly after the multiplication of the loaves, moreover, "he went off into the hills to pray until dawn." In the olive grove of Gethsemane, Jesus entered the garden with three disciples, but left them behind, going off to pray alone—to offer his prayer in the face of death.

Mark does tell us of Jesus' actual prayer in Gethsemane and of his final prayer on the cross. Though Jesus offers us no methods of prayer, he does teach us how to pray in his words to his Father at the end of his life. Every Christian knows Jesus' prayer of agony, "Abba, all things are possible for you. Take this cup from me. Yet not what I will, but what you will." And Jesus' final prayer at the moment of death—"My God, my God, why have you forsaken me?"—has heralded our redemption through twenty centuries.

Luke and John record Jesus' prayer at greater length than Mark. Yet, whether his actual prayer was recorded or not, we know that from the beginning to the end of his life, Jesus was always a man of prayer. It is not surprising that his prayers were not always written down. The evangelists presented Jesus as the Messiah and as the Evangelizer, the bearer of good news, as the man who went about doing good. And John tells us finally, "There were many other things that Jesus did; if all were written down, the world itself, I suppose, would not hold all the books that would have to be written."

But there is another aspect of Jesus' prayer not so often

spoken of by biblical commentators. Jesus was a man of the East. Silent interior prayer is the deepest intuition of Eastern spirituality. Jesus put his interior communion with the Father into words for us when he gave us the gift of the Lord's Prayer. This is the prayer that he lived, the prayer through which he taught us how to pray.[2] His whole life was his prayer to the Father. Jesus' prayer at the Last Supper was his prayer for all of us to the Father. And his prayer on the cross proved that what he lived for and what he died for were the same: complete acceptance of the will of his Father.

It has been pointed out over and over again that at Jesus' death the Father was silent.[3] Out of this silence came resurrection. And so, "the ultimate prayer of Jesus was silence" (Ignatius of Antioch). His silence was most notable when his experience of his mission on earth appeared inexplicable to human beings.

While Jesus was a man of prayer, his prayer was always beyond formalities and rituals. Neither concept nor logic can clarify his silent communion with the Father. In this context, we may note once again that Eastern forms of prayer are directed dominantly and ultimately toward wordless union with God in the Spirit. Whether Indian women and men are Christian or Hindu, the silence of the cross is meaningful to them. The crucial meeting point of Eastern and Western prayer is "the cave of the heart" where the Spirit dwells. How else can we account for the millions of Hindus who choose to worship Christ as their "avatar" or incarnation of the Lord? At the Last Supper, Jesus was supremely conscious of the need for his apostles to understand that his Spirit was *within them*:

> I shall ask the Father and he will give you another Advocate to be with you forever, that Spirit of truth whom the world can never receive since it neither sees nor knows him; but you know him, because he is with you, he is in

you. . . . I am in the Father and you in me and I in you
(Jn 14:16–17, 20).

Thousands of years before the birth of Christ, the East
knew through cosmic revelation that the Spirit of God lives in
the hearts of men and women. The revelation of the mystery
of the redemption, the resurrection, and the Trinity awaited
the incarnation of the unique Christ. This mystery unites all
men and women of East and West in the dynamic love of Father and Son experienced everlastingly in the Holy Spirit. The
scriptural prayer of Jesus was most often a prayer of silence,
not only because his loving communion with the Father is inexpressible but because he knew that the union of his followers
with his own Spirit could be expressed completely only in silent interior communion.

2. Eastern Scripture as a Way of Prayer—The Upanishads

Many Western Christians today are reading the Hindu
Scriptures as a ground for meditation. To be sure, some Westerners are attracted by mere substitutes for spiritual experience: Eastern and psychedelic cults in false versions which
promise "overnight mysticism." Yet a younger generation in
the West is seeking true spiritual experience of Eastern ways
of scriptural prayer under the guidance of competent directors.
They have discovered, surprisingly, that the long-ago Age of
the Upanishads resembled in a certain sense the West of the
1980's! That age was marked by a questioning of rites, myths,
and theological reasoning apparently not related to their actual
religious experience. A malaise developed from failure of dialogue between a rising generation and representatives of or-

ganized religion. There was a need for change of structures of worship, yet a fear of the disappearance of old structures. The *Upanishads* spoke to the spiritual hunger of the young.

In the era of the 1980's, in which we are finally beginning to respond to the outstanding religious traditions of the past, a meeting of the great religions of the world seems inevitable. The contemporary Western world is rejecting a religion of "words, words, words." It knows that spiritual life is made up of neither formulas nor logical conclusions. It recognizes the need for meditation and silence in prayer; it also recognizes that communion with God in the depths of one's being is beyond both silence and non-silence. The message of God comes to us through Scripture, God's word, through the holy person who has himself experienced communion with God, and through our own experience. And the people of God hear the word of God through the visible Church when it speaks the truth of God.

Christians are finding that contemplative reading of the sacred texts of the Hindus often leads to surprising correlations with their reading of the Bible and with their own experience of God. They are discovering the mysteries that God revealed long ago to other races that were never promised a Redeemer. The Hindu Scriptures read most profitably by Christians today are the major *Upanishads* and the *Bhagavadgita*. The most important texts of the two great epics, the *Mahabharata* and the *Ramayana*, are also found to be valuable for meditation. And the writings of Indian saints and sages appeal to many Westerners: Ramakrishna, Vivekananda, Ramana Maharishi, and Mahatma Gandhi. Certain correlations of the above writings with Christian Scripture develop naturally from the spiritual experience of the Christian reader. Because the *Bhagavadgita* is an interpersonal dialogue between Lord Krishna and his follower, Arjuna, it is perhaps the best Eastern approach to and prefiguration of God's revelation of the personal God in the New Testament. The *Gita* is a source of personal theism in India.

Although the personal God is not dominant in Hindu spirituality, beautiful examples of a response to a personal God and of human interdependence are found in well-known stories of southern India, where the saint, Ramanuja, was the great leader of the followers of the god Vishnu.

The story is told that Ramanuja once received spiritual initiation from a famous *sannyasi*, who told him that he must never repeat to anyone the sacred prayer, or *mantra*, he was given for meditation. It was most holy, and it would give to whoever repeated it the grace of enlightenment. To the teacher's dismay Ramanuja immediately called one and all—even members of the "untouchable" caste—to receive from him the "priceless jewel" of his *mantra*. All who heard him were filled with spiritual joy. Confronted by his outraged guru, Ramanuja explained, "Sir, I knew that to repeat this *mantra* was a great sin. I disobeyed your command only because I was ready to suffer the pangs of hell. If I go to hell and thousands of men and women are thereby able to go to heaven, what could be more fortunate?" The teacher, realizing his disciple's great-heartedness, embraced him warmly.

Even though a Christian need not make an academic study of Hindu Scripture to appreciate its value in prayer, an understanding of certain Hindu terms is valuable as an initiation to prayer in the Indian sacred texts.[4]

Brahma refers to the Absolute God beyond all relationship, the creative source of all that is. *Brahma* is one alone, a non-dual mystery. Only faith can perceive *Brahma*, though the power and freedom of *Brahma* is revealed in all beings.

Upanishad means literally to be seated at the feet of a spiritual master and to receive instruction. It refers to mysterious teaching which is a disclosure of certain spiritual "correspondences" perceptible at an intuitive but not at a mental level. The whole universe is believed to be made up of correspondences. In the Christian context, for example, Christ himself is a mystery of pure relation to the Father and the Spirit.

Atman can best be described in Western terms, perhaps, as an attempt to indicate that which makes an individual to be himself or herself. It refers to one's essential personal identity. In the *Upanishads*, one reaches the *Atman* not by external action but by continual interiorization. The ultimate experience of Upanishadic correlations is the discovery of the deepest center of the self which is *Atman* and the deepest center of the universe which is *Brahma*. The experience is not rational; it is an intuition, "a flash of light," an awakening to oneself and to God which lights up consciousness or "the space of the heart."

In this final state of realization, the Hindu believes that no distinction between the knower and the known remains. The Christian in union with God, however, is always aware of communion. Even in total absorption in the Divine, the sense of personal identity is never lost. While the person is other than he or she was before the gift of mystical communion with God, "he continues to live even though a part of him belongs to another world."

The *Upanishads* are a written record of spiritual experience intended to lead to the realization of God in the very ground of one's being.[5] This experience can be expressed only in metaphors, similes, or analogical terms intended to communicate, as far as possible, a direct intuition. The *guru*, the one who has known this experience of God, is able to initiate the disciple into the teaching of the *Upanishads*. Since the experience is indefinable, it is often expressed in negative terms: "not this, not that." When it is known, all is known: it transcends ordinary consciousness. One word that points to it is *saccidananda*, which means being, awareness, bliss.

This mystical experience has been proclaimed consistently by holy men and women of the East over thousands of years. It has been a continual source of philosophy, art, and spiritual life. It is a decisive experience of humanity. Christian mystics often describe it in terms similar to those of the East. Yet the Christian God is always a personal God. For the Christian, the bliss of mystical experience exists in the Holy Spirit. Only through the Trinity can the mystery be named.

The Christian mystic Abhishiktananda points out that the Prologue to the Gospel of St. John recalls the teaching of the *Upanishads*. The Spirit is in the heart of every person, waiting for the moment when he or she is ready to hear the voice of the Spirit. All who receive the light of the Spirit have access to divine mystery, to the glory of the unique Son. In fact, all that is said of this divine mystery in the *Upanishads* was said of Jesus Christ before his incarnation. Reading the *Upanishads* can help the Christian to enter into a deeper and more experiential knowledge of his own Holy Scripture.[6] What the Upanishads present in terms of being, Christian Scripture presents in terms of the gifts and fruits of the Holy Spirit. The mystery of the Spirit in the depths of the Father comes to fruition in the New Testament. And the call of the Spirit comes to all men and women in the midst of existence in time, whether it be the age of the Upanishads, of Christ, or of the present century. Everything in the universe exists in one totality. Redemption is not past or future. It is now.

Practice: Hindu Scriptural Prayer for Christians[7]

1. In reading the *Upanishads* or the *Bhagavadgita*, your goal is to discover the correlation between your own experience of God and the mysteries revealed long ago through cosmic revelation to people of another tradition.

2. Do not *study* the Hindu scriptural texts, but read them again and again. Meditate upon them. Classifying and categorizing ideas will be of no help in scriptural prayer. The Hindu guru teaches that hearing, reflecting, and meditating upon Scripture will release the meaning of the symbols and thus reach a profound level of the human heart.

3. Do not concentrate on your own thoughts while reading Hindu Scripture. Thinking about yourself impedes the flash of illumination from the text. We tend to read and hear through our own mental make-up, our own culture, our own ideas of society. Thus we are in danger of substituting a particular expression of experience for the spiritual insight offered by the scriptural text.

4. Follow three main phases in reading Hindu Scripture:

   Read from the *Upanishads* or the *Gita* with openness to new experience acquired through a contemplative approach to the texts.

   Meditate on the relevance of your experience to your own Christian faith.

   Be open to new forms of prayer suggested by your new experience. Let the experience find its own form of prayer. Trust in the Holy Spirit as the center of your own being.

Practice: A Hindu-Christian Scriptural Prayer Service[8]

1. Prayerful reading of Hindu and Christian Scripture has as its goal an inward assimilation of God's message under the guidance of the Holy Spirit.

2. Preparation for the Reading of Scripture

Calm your mind and have a listening heart.

Silence instinctive egoism which may urge you to impose your own views even in the holiest matters, thus drowning out the voice of the Spirit.

Allow yourself to be open to the word of God, to the unpredictable suggestions with which Scripture may confront you.

Have a firm purpose of "metanoia" or conversion.

3. Steps in Group Practice of Reading Scripture

Several minutes of calm recollection.

An opening prayer drawn from Christian tradition.

A reading from the *Old* or the *New Testament*.

Brief commentary on the reading from a member of the group, aimed at bringing out essential points for Christians open to the action of the Holy Spirit.

Fifteen minutes of silence spent in reflecting on the text in the presence of Christ or in simply being silently aware of Christ.

Sharing of the thoughts of participants. The contemplative character of the reading within the fellowship of the Church is essential. The basic attitude of the group is that of listening to and questioning the Spirit speaking within one another. "Before speaking ourselves, we must first listen with great attention to the other man's words, and even more to his heart" (Paul VI, *Ecclesiam Suam*).

A reading from the *Upanishads* in the same manner as above. The voice of God sounds throughout the universe and the whole of time, fills the hearts of men and women, and is heard in the unfolding of human history. People who lived before the birth of Jesus were "not merely learning about but experiencing God" (Thomas Aquinas).

In reading the *Upanishads*, forget dogma and theology. Reading Scripture is not a course in comparative religion. Listen to the Spirit speaking through Indian spiritual experience.

Remember that all that luminous in the Scriptures of India was placed there by the Spirit in preparation for the coming of Christ. We do not know the mystery of Christ in whom "the whole fullness of the Godhead dwells bodily" (Col 2:9).

Your passage from Indian scriptural prayer to the glory of God in Christ requires faith. Are you a living witness of God's glory?

After listening to the Spirit speaking in the responses of the group to the *Upanishads* center yourself in the Spirit within you in silence.

Readings from the Upanishads for Christians

O Thou that art manifest, be Thou manifest to us:
From the unreal, lead us to the Real;
From darkness lead us to Light;
From death lead us to Immortality.
            (*Brihad Aranyaka Upanishad, 1,3*)

Knowledge has its place, and so has ignorance;
this have we learned from the men of old
who distinguished them for us.
When knowledge and ignorance
both alike have been transcended,
only then does a man pass to the further shore of death . . .
and attain to immortality.

                              (*Isa Upanishad*)

The infinite is happiness.
There is no happiness in anything small.
Only the infinite is happiness.
But one must desire to understand the infinite.
When one sees nothing else,
understands nothing else,
that is the infinite.
But where one sees something else,
hears something else,
understands something else,
that is the small. . . .
                    (Chandogya Upanishad, VII 23, 24)

In the sheath of gold is Brahman,
pure, undivided; he is brilliant,
the light of lights. . . .
In him the sun does not shine,
nor the moon, nor the stars,
nor does the lightning flash.
He shines, and all things draw their light from him.
In his light everything becomes luminous.
                    (Mundaka Upanishad, II, 2, 9–10)

The light that shines beyond all things on earth,
beyond us all, beyond the heavens,
beyond the highest, the very highest heaven,
this is the light that shines in our hearts.
                    (Chandogya Upanishad, III 13, 14)

The face of truth is covered as with a golden disc.
Unveil it, O Creator of the light,
that we who love the truth may see it. . . .
Spread forth your rays and gather up your radiant light,
That we may behold you in your loveliest form.
                    (Katha Upanishad, V 15)
                    (Isha Upanishad, 17–18)

Lead us to a world of freedom, O Wise One.
Lead us to heavenly light, to fearlessness and peace.
Strong is your arm, O powerful God.
We take refuge in you.
May the atmosphere we breathe, breathe in us fearlessness,
Fearlessness on earth, fearlessness in heaven,
Fearlessness above and below, in front and behind.
O Power of God, grant us freedom from all fear.
May we be without fear of friend or foe,
free from fear of the known and the unknown,
free from fear by night and day.
May all the world be free from fear.

(Hymn from the *Vedas*)

When all desires that cling to the heart are surrendered,
then a mortal becomes immortal,
and even in this world he becomes one with God.
When all the ties that bind the heart are unloosed,
then a mortal becomes immortal. This is sacred teaching.

(*Katha Upanishad*, VI, 12–15)

That one is Brahman, the Supreme, the Unchanging.
He is life; he is speech; he is spirit;
He is the Real; he is Immortality.
It is he who is the mark to aim at.
My dear, aim straight for that mark.
Take into your hands the shining bow of the Upanishads.
On it set your arrow
sharpened by meditation.
With your mind stretched toward union, bend that bow.
My dear, aim at that mark. It is he, the Unchanging.

(Mundaka Upanishad, II, 2)

He who offers to me with devotion, says the Lord,
only a leaf or a flower, or a fruit, or even a little water,
this I accept from the yearning soul
because with a pure heart it is offered with love.

Whatever you do or eat, or give or offer in adoration,
let it be an offering to me, my child.
Whatever you suffer, suffer it for me. . . .
Those who worship me with devotion,
they are in me and I in them.

Fix your mind on me, give me your heart
and your sacrifice and your adoration.
This is my word supreme: You shall in truth come to me,
for you are dear to me.

Leave all things behind,
and come to me for your salvation.
I will set you free from the bondage of sin.
Fear no more.

                    (*Gita*, 9, 26–27: 18, 65–66)

Who is my true devotee? Says the Lord:
He who has no thought of self,
who has good will for all creatures,
Who is friendly with all and full of compassion,
even-minded in pain and pleasure, and who is forgiving.

The yogi ever content and full of my joy, says the Lord,
whose soul is in harmony, whose determination is strong,
whose mind and inner vision are set on me,
he is my true devotee and he is dear to me.

He whose peace is not shaken by others,
and before whom others find peace,
beyond excitement and anger or fear;
he is my true devotee and he is dear to me.

He who is free from vain expectations and is pure,
who is wise and knows what to do,
who in inner peace watches both sides,
who fears not, who works not for himself but for God,
this man loves me and he is dear to me.

                    (*Gita*, 12, 13–16)

Who is my true devotee? Says the Lord:
He who is beyond excitement and repulsion.
who complains not and lusts not for things,
who remains unmoved by good and evil fortune
and who has love, he is dear to me.

I love the man who is even-minded to friend and foe,
whose heart is at peace in honor and disgrace,
in heat and cold, pleasure and pain,
who is free from the chain of attachments.

The man who remains the same in blame and in praise,
whose heart is quiet, who is happy with whatever he has,
whose home is not this world
and who has love, he is dear to me.

But even dearer to me is he who has faith and love,
and who has me as his end supreme,
he who hears my word of truth
and who comes to the waters of everlasting life.

(Gita, 12, 17–20)

Hear again my word supreme,
the deepest secret heard only in the silence of the heart.
Because I love you
I speak to you words of salvation.

Give your mind to me, give me your heart,
and your sacrifice and your adoration. . . .
You shall in truth come to me, for you are dear to me.
Give up all things and turn to me, your only refuge.
I will deliver you from all evils, fear no more.

(Gita, 18, 64–66)

Offer in your heart all your works to me,
and see me as the fulfillment of your love.
Take refuge in loving contemplation
and always rest your soul in me.

If your heart finds rest in me,
by my grace you shall overcome all dangers;
but if your thoughts are on yourself
and you will not listen, you shall perish. . . .

God dwells in the hearts of all beings, beloved,
your God dwells in your heart
and his power of wonder moves all things . . .
whirling them onwards on the stream of time. . . .

I have given you words of vision and wisdom
more secret than hidden mysteries.
Ponder them in the silence of your heart,
and then, in freedom, do your will.

(Gita, 18, 57–63)

NOTES

1. Donald Senior, "Prayer According to Mark," *Praying,* Spring 1985, pp. 7–12.

2. Lucien Legrand, "Prayer in the Bible," *Praying Seminar,* pp. 72–73.

3. Joseph Pathrapankal, "Characteristics of the Prayer of Jesus," *Praying Seminar,* pp. 78–80.

4. Abhishiktananda, *The Further Shore,* pp. 76–77, 92–95.

5. Bede Griffiths, *Vedanta and Christian Faith,* Los Angeles, The Dawn Horse Press, 1973, pp. 7–14.

6. Abhishiktananda, *Hindu-Christian Meeting Point,* pp. 83–90.

7. Abhishiktananda, *Towards the Renewal of the Indian Church,* pp. 53–54, 57–59.

8. Abhishiktananda, *Hindu-Christian Meeting Point,* pp. 26–30.

SUGGESTED READINGS

Acharya, Francis. *Prayer with the Harp of the Spirit*, Vol. I. Bangalore, India: Kurisumala Ashram and Asian Trading Corporation, 1980.

Amalorpavadoss, D.S. *Gospel and Culture: Evangelization and Inculturation*. Bangalore, India: NBCLC, 1978.

Amalorpavadoss, D.S. *Research Seminar on Non-Biblical Scriptures*. Bangalore, India: NBCLC, 1974.

Amalorpavadoss, D.S., ed. *Towards Indigenisation in the Liturgy*. Bangalore, India: NBCLC, 1973.

Colaco, J.M., ed. *Jesus Christ in Asian Suffering and Hope*. Madras: Christian Literature Society, 1977.

Comblin, José. *Sent from the Father: Meditations on the Fourth Gospel*. Maryknoll, New York: Orbis Books, 1979.

Neuner, Joseph, ed. *Christian Revelation and World Religions*. London: Burns and Oates, 1967.

Thomas, M.M. *The Acknowledged Christ of the Indian Renaissance*. Madras: Christian Literature Society, 1970.

Upanishads. With Commentary by S. Radhakrishnan. London: Allen and Unwin, 1953. New York: Penguin Books, 1965. New York: New American Library, Mentor Book. 1981.

V I

Prayer Through Art:
Symbol and Icon

Everyone has heard the statement, "Prayer is art, and art is prayer." Like many clever metaphors, it contains a half-truth. We know that creation is an expression of the beauty of God. The first artist "saw all that he had made, and it was very good." And in Exodus we read that the Creator "filled man with the Spirit of God and endowed him with skill and perception and knowledge of every kind of craft: for the art of designing and working in gold and silver and bronze, for cutting stones to be set, for carving in wood."

In a certain sense, the artist repeats at his own level the creative activity of God: he seeks reality beyond appearance. Similarly, when a person responds to a work of art, he repeats, to a certain degree, the experience of the artist.[1] Thus art is "the twin of mystical experience." Yet a simple equation of religious experience and art is not satisfying, even to the Eastern mind which often finds analogy and metaphor more satisfying than logical syllogisms.

Famous Hindu philosopher T.M.P. Mahadevan points out that art experience, unlike God experience, lasts only a brief time; moreover, it is "artificially" produced, from outside the person, by the work of art itself.[2] Spiritual experience is a gift of God, known "within the core of the heart." Yet most of us would agree that true religious experience is basically artistic and that art can play a role in the development of our spiritual life, sometimes even an indispensable role in leading certain persons to God.

Hindus have varied opinions as to how a person finally experiences God, perhaps after a long struggle. Some call it an intuition; others call it "a flash of light." An Indian parable perhaps illustrates best the awakening of the interior self:

> Ten slow-witted men, crossing a stream, check on their number to make sure that all are safe. Each tries to count, but finds only nine because he leaves himself out. Seeing them all weeping, a kind traveler in another boat tells each one: "You are the tenth." Each experiences an immediate conviction: "I am the tenth."

We may eventually become aware of experience of God after a long struggle, just as we may recognize the unique value of a work of great art.

Because religion and art both have their sources in the beauty of God, the great mystics of East and West have often been artists. History offers us magnificent examples of spiritual artists, from the Indian authors of the *Upanishads* and the *Bhagavadgita* to the writers of the Old and New Testaments, to Teresa of Avila, John of the Cross, and countless saints. According to Hindu tradition, the artist or sculptor should also be a *yogi*, a holy person experienced in contemplation. The artist, by his or her nature, leads men and women to spiritual serenity and joy. Art reveals the glory of God in cosmic art forms, and may become a source of grace: art and spirituality may become interdependent. Great art, in its transcendent vision, moves human beings toward union with God.[3]

Christian mystics, Western as well as Eastern, have always made art an aid to prayer. The Hindu artist who created an image of God was exhorted to "meditate on the God whose image he was fashioning." Similarly, the Christian tradition was manifested in music, painting, and the great cathedrals of Europe. Religious art in medieval Europe, as well as the East, was an act of worship. The artist who created the icon as an image of Christ and Mary was worshiping the Lord:

> The wood is chosen and blessed, the paint is blessed, the artist prepares himself by fasting, confession, and communion. He keeps ascetical rules while working, and when his work is completed, it is blessed. By the power of the Holy Spirit, the icon becomes more than a painting. It is filled with presence, imbued with the grace of the Spirit, and linked with the saint it represents through the mystery of the communion of saints and the cosmic unity of all things.

In the monastery of St. Mark in Florence, the frescoes of Fra Angelico were designed to recreate the mystery of salvation. St. Teresa of Avila wrote of a figure of Jesus so striking that it disturbed her soul and led her to Christ. St. John of the Cross sketched images of Jesus and the saints as he meditated. One of his most creative drawings of Christ on the cross inspired a famous modern painting of the crucifixion by Salvador Dali.

Among Hindus, both today and in the past, the gesture and grace of yogic meditation are drawn from the depths of the soul. The spiritual is expressed in cosmic art forms that concentrate on the source of life in the Divine. Indeed, one has only to visit the ancient temple of Banaras or the temple in Madurai, Tamil Nadu, to be aware of unforgettable spiritual beauty. Inspired Indian art, sacred art, confronts existential truth. Lived reality and transcendent symbol become one. The visitor becomes aware of "holy space." People of all castes find their spiritual desires satisfied. Moreover, the levels on which Hindu artistic images function have been compared with stages of contemplation in Hindu spirituality: "waking, dreaming, and deep sleep." And these stages have also been compared, concomitantly, with the stages of the spiritual life spoken of by the Western Christian mystics: active and passive purgation, illumination, and union.

As Christians, we know that Jesus, the image of the invisible God, delighted in the beauty of his Father's creation. He loved the birds of the air, the flowers of the field, the countryside of Galilee. The author of the Sermon on the Mount was a literary genius. The speaker of the farewell words at the Last Supper was a poet. He praised his Father with his whole being. His art opened women and men to the Infinite.

The human thirst for the invisible God was completely satisfied only when Christ assumed a visible human form. Jesus himself is our model for complete worship of the Father. The greatest beauty of the human being lies in the soul in which the Spirit lives. Men and women are therefore called to express their worship of God with their whole being: senses, body, emotion, mind, spirit.

One wonders, then, why the senses and the emotions have sometimes been given so little place in many Western Christian ways of prayer, while effort of the will has sometimes been considered not only the central but the only path to holiness. Temperaments of people differ: for some, emotions and feelings play a primary role, especially in the early stages of prayer life. They are a first stage in the journey to interiority. Where faith is strong and deep, it often finds natural expression in art—in poetry, painting, sculpture, music, and dance.

Why, then, is the joy of spiritual art so often reserved to the minority of the faithful? When we pray, our natural tendency is to respond to God with our whole selves. Worship itself is symbolic. Prayer without artistic symbol can become a shell without substance. We all know that the liturgy, when it is dry, wordy, and abstract, does not lead us easily to contemplation. And when music is secondary or ornamental, it is not usually integral to our worship.

Authentic art is often absent from the spiritual lives of many Christians.[4] Romanesque and Gothic cathedrals are largely a thing of the past. Today we frequently use multi-purpose, functional assembly halls as churches. Except for sacramental symbols, little that is symbolic is found in these churches. True, a greater effort has been made since Vatican II to improve the art of both our churches and our liturgies. But we still have a long way to go.

The Westerner visiting India becomes suddenly aware of the mediocrity of Christian church architecture side by side with the artistic magnificence of Hindu temples throughout the land. Based on Western models of the late nineteenth or early twentieth century, many Christian churches in India reflect the Western tendency to neglect the expression of the whole person in worship. The individual's craving for the beauty of creation in worship is thus repressed because of a lack of openness to the highest manifestations of spiritual beauty in art.

Yet true art does persist in Eastern Christian worship. The icon is an excellent example. An icon is more than an image; it is a focus of real presence. There is a mysterious link between an icon of Christ and Christ himself. The icon participates in "the energies of Christ as the active power of Christ working for salvation." This mysterious power inspires med-

itation. Hindu poet Rabindranath Tagore expresses an analogous thought:

> We have eternal sources within us. The hidden way that
> leads down to this source, the path of meditation and
> prayer and contemplation, and the vessel in which the wa-
> ter of life is brought up from the source is art. The vessel
> may have many shapes: words, songs, gestures, dance,
> colors, or material forms.

The poet is magnificently aware of the Spirit within the souls
of men and women.

The difference between Tagore's interpretation of spiritual art and the Christian's is that the Christian image is clearly
incarnational. St. John the Evangelist's bold affirmation of the
new creation in Christ who became flesh offers a spiritual and
artistic image unique in nature. An Indian Christian artist,
Jyoti Sahi, points out that after the resurrection we can no
longer look upon the human body as something wholly of
death. The purpose of Christian art, he declares, is surely to
search for meaning in the resurrected body. The Christian artist must discover in the human body the seed not only of lim-
itation and death but also of life and liberation.[5] Sahi suggests
that the body of Christ, in which the seed of resurrection was
implanted, is Mary, in whom the Word became flesh. The
body of Christ was derived wholly from the body of Mary in
unique fashion. Thus early Eastern Christian icons, while
stressing the incarnation, often center upon the image of Mary.
Her icon was venerated as "not made by hands." The earliest
icon, at least according to tradition, was the icon of Mary
painted by St. Luke. Thus tradition names as first Christian
artist the evangelist who linked the role of Christ as priest with
the founding of the Church. While Mary has been a model for
Western Christian artists for centuries, she has seldom been

presented as "the body of Christ" in precisely the sense of the icons of the Eastern Church.

A digression may demonstrate the attitude of many Easterners, including thousands of non-Christians, toward Mary as mother of God. A foreigner in India is often amazed to see Indians of all faiths—Christians, Hindus, Muslims—bowing before the icon of Mary. One day the writer spoke with a Hindu rickshaw driver in Bangalore, south India, who displayed an icon of Mary in his car. She asked him if Mary represented to him a goddess like the Hindu "Earth Mother," Kali. With a laugh, the man responded, "No. She is Mary, the mother of Jesus Christ, and she answers our prayers." On feast days, when festivals are held at shrines of Mary in Madras and other Indian cities, hundreds of Hindus, in greater number than Christians, come to honor the mother of God. Western Christians in the twentieth century are sometimes troubled by the concept of devotion to Mary at the possible expense of worship of Christ. It is ironic that Hindus should understand the place of Mary in the economy of salvation better than many Christians. Their understanding is not logical or conceptual: it is a grace of the heart.

Many Hindus who have emigrated to the West quietly pray to Jesus, Mary and the Christian saints while confirmed in Hinduism as their religion. The concept of "conversion" is strange to them. Speaking to a Hindu engineer in a large eastern city in the United States, for example, the writer remarked that hundreds of Hindus in India worship Jesus Christ. The engineer smiled and answered, "Not hundreds. Millions! I worship an image of Christ in my home every day." Hindus know that there is one God alone. "God is one, but his names are many."

Practice of Prayer through Art: The Rosary as Meditation

Mary as mother, as woman of history, as archetype, as the body of Christ represents a series of icons related to the life of Jesus.

The rosary of Mary, as a practice of meditation in which visualized images are called forth, is centered in the repeated invocation of Mary. Unfortunately, the rosary in the West has become in many instances a kind of repetitive technique of prayer. It can become, unintentionally, a shell without substance. In Eastern Christianity, the threefold series of images—joyful, sorrowful, glorious—is pictured in fifteen icons which provide a focus for real presence, for a mysterious relationship between the icon of Mary and Mary herself. The salutation of the angel at the annunciation provides the chief mantra, or mystical form of invocation: "Rejoice, so highly favored! The Lord is with you." The *namjapa* repeats itself so as to become eventually an unchanging part of the consciousness of the one who prays.

Mary is the sacred icon in relation to the body of Jesus. Christ is the Word. He gives the icon its meaning and dynamism. In Indian terminology, he leads the worshiper from the unreal to the Real. Christ himself is the door through which the icon must pass to attain true vision. Ultimately, the Christian image aspires to the revelation of Mount Tabor, where the disciples, passing from darkness to light, see Christ as he really is. On Tabor their vision is at last able to grasp him.

This seeing in spirit and truth foreshadows the reality of the resurrection. In the icons of the glorious mysteries of the rosary, the resurrection is not something in the future as it is in the joyful annunciation. Christ is risen. This was the great proclamation of the kerygma. "Here in the heart of a world which we see imperfectly with our imperfect senses, the resurrection is already reality." It is our own eyes that cannot see.

But the resurrection is realized here and now by those who see with the light of the Spirit within them. "Into this resurrection the mother of Christ is already received." To see the icon of Mary as a symbol which is more than image, which embodies Christ mysteriously within itself, is to pray the rosary with the vision of our whole being. It is to enter into contemplation of the Divine.

NOTES

1. M. Hiriyanna, "Art Experience," *Radhakrishnan*, eds. W.R. Inge, *et al.*, London, 1951, 178–79.
2. T.M.P. Mahadevan, *The Philosophy of Beauty*, Bombay, 1969.
3. James Thamburaj, "Prayer and Indian Art," *Praying Seminar*, pp. 222–28.
4. Michael Amaladoss, "Art and Spirituality in India," *Indian Spirituality in Action*, pp. 142–50.
5. Jyoti Sahi, "Prayer and Indian Art," *Praying Seminar*, pp. 229–35.

SUGGESTED READINGS

Amaladoss, Michael. "Art and Spirituality in Action," in *Indian Spirituality in Action*. Bombay: Asian Trading Corporation, 1973.

Coomeraswamy, Ananda. *The Dance of Siva*. Bombay: Asian Trading Corporation, 1948.

Hiriyanna, M. *Art Experience*. Mysore, India: Kavyalaya Publishers, 1954.

Irudayaraj, Xavier. "Art and Ministries," in D.S. Amalorpavadoss, ed., *Ministries in the Church in India*. New Delhi: C.B.C.I. Centre, 1976.

Lederle, Matthew. "Interpreting Christ Through Indian Art," in *Indian Spirituality in Action*. Bombay: Asian Trading Corporation, 1973.

Mahadevan, T.M.P. *The Philosophy of Beauty*. Bombay: Bharatiya Vidya Bhavan, 1969.

Rayan, Samuel. "Christ Had Imagination," *Jeevadhara*, II (1972), 210–21.

Taylor, R.W. "Some Interpretations of Jesus in Indian Painting," *Religion and Society*, XVII (1970), 78–106.

Zimmer, Heinrich. *Myths and Symbols in Indian Art and Civilization*. New York: Harper, 1946.

VII

Ashram Prayer: Christian and Hindu

———————

The ancient practice by which the Hindu *sannyasi* or holy men retreated to a secluded dwelling to pray and to contemplate is perhaps the unique source of monasticism in the world. It goes back as far as Buddha and the *Upanishads*. The ashram is not comparable to a traditional Western monastery. Nor is it a house of prayer with the title *Ashram* on the door. Rather, it is a place in which a holy person lives and in which disciples gather who choose him as their guru in order to learn the way to experience of God. It is founded not on land but in the heart of the guru who lives in union with the Divine. When a guru dies, the ashram may simply go out of existence.

Ashram life is based on the tradition of the *sannyasi* who lived in renunciation and dedication to the Lord in order to achieve *moksha*, which is salvation or liberation. The goal of the guru was to be freed from reincarnation, the cycle of birth and death, and thus to attain *saccidananda* or "being, pure consciousness, and unending bliss."

Historically, both the *sannyasi* and *sadhu*, or mendicant ascetic, maintained their tradition of renunciation in an unbroken line. Over the years, traditions were preserved by different religious groups within *mutts*, or monasteries. Of the modern *mutts*, the best known are those established by Ramakrishna in the nineteenth century and perpetuated by his famous disciple, Vivekananda. These Hindu monasteries, as well as Eastern Christian monasteries, have offered to historians a fascinating comparison with the monasteries developed in the Christian West.

There still exist in India today small retreats in out-of-the-way places, usually at the foot of mountains or beside sacred rivers, which resemble in every way the ashrams of ancient times. The ashram tradition is between two and three thousand years old, but it is as living, perhaps, as it has ever been. In their forest retreats the ancient *sannyasi* taught the truths that eventually became embodied in the *Upanishads*. They taught of the One Absolute God: "All this is Brahman. From it the universe comes forth, into it the universe merges, and in it the universe breathes."[1]

The ashrams where holy men lived the spiritual life in the past are revered as sacred places, often visited by pilgrims. The *sadhus*, or wandering holy men who spend their lives in prayer and meditation, begging for food, come to these holy places to find peace.

The living quarters of the *sannyasi* are always simple. He may live, for example, in a small, porch-like building with canvas screens, and sleep on a small mat covered with a leopard skin. Pictures of the god Siva or of Krishna may be the only furnishings of his tiny room.

We usually discover in speaking with a *sannyasi* that he has lived years of spiritual discipline in pursuing his chosen *sadhana*, or way to God. He has studied and lived by the teaching of the *Bhagavadgita*. He will tell us that a lifetime of faithfulness is the price of experiencing Reality. And he will insist on the supreme importance of an interior desire to know God: "Every smallest incident of life can be a help on the way, if you have an inner desire for spiritual advancement. If you don't have the inner desire, even happenings of major importance cannot lead you on."

John Moffitt, a former Ramakrishna monk who is now a Christian, tells of visiting a *sannyasi* in the sacred town of Puri, Orissa, and listening to his teaching. A monk asked the *sannyasi* a traditional question concerning the search for the spiritual ideal: "What is the way?" The holy man responded, "What do *you* say?" And the monk replied, "Devotion to the Lord." The sannyasi then spoke gently of the importance of self-surrender to God. Here we have a beautiful example of how the *sannyasi* does not interfere with the spiritual direction, in this case *bhakti marga*, chosen by a person seeking liberation. The same *sannyasi*, questioned as to whether he was praying for the welfare of India, answered, "Why India alone? The whole universe! All are one." The true holy one reveals in all his conversation that knowing God is enough.

Today the Hindu *sannyasi*, like the Buddhist monk, has become a world phenomenon, attracting a vast number of young people of the West who seek *experience of* God rather than *knowledge about* God. Gurus and yogis, each teaching his own method of meditation and asceticism, have large followings in almost every country in the world. To be sure, there are false prophets among them, as among all religious teachers, but many of them teach their *sadhanas*, or ways to God, without prejudice, encouraging their followers to remain committed to the faiths in which they were born. Most Hindus, while accepting great freedom in religious beliefs, do not approve of conversion to another religion as such.

The way of life of the Hindu *sannyasi* exerts a strong influence on many Indian Christians today. Especially since Vatican Council II, Christian ashrams have sprung up all over the Indian subcontinent. The famous Christian mystic Abhishiktananda (Henri Le Saux) predicted that three main branches of *sannyasi* will develop in Christian India.[2]

The first will be purely contemplative. People of prayer will live alone or in small groups, preferably in the sacred places of India consecrated by centuries of holy living. They will seek the sacred quiet, the prayer of silence of the ancient ashrams.

The second type of *sannyasi* will feel the call to minister to his brothers' and sisters' needs, to teach them the path which leads to the Spirit in the "guha," or "cave of the heart." This *sannyasi* will attempt to preach like Jesus of Galilee, but not yet like Peter on Pentecost Day, who asked his listeners to be baptized in Christ. Baptism for the Hindu who was never promised a Redeemer will be delayed or regarded as secondary. The Hindu who accepts baptism may be completely disowned by his family and caste. Many missioners therefore believe it to be wiser to delay baptism until a group of Hindus can accept the sacraments together, offering one another the support they have lost.

The third type of Christian *sannyasi* will attempt to recapture the spirit that animated St. Francis of Assisi and his first companions. These mendicants will wander in poverty from village to town, living on alms, singing their love for the Lord, and calling all to share in their joy.

Among all *sannyasis*, no matter what the type, life will revolve around the ideals of simplicity, poverty, prayer, worship, and the orientation of each day toward personal contemplation under spiritual direction. The *bramachari*, or student, will learn holiness through personal relationship with the guru who is holy, who has experienced God.

Practice of Ashram Prayer for Christians

The following practices of ashram life suitable for contemporary Eastern or Western Christians are based on a description proposed by Bede Griffiths, an English Benedictine mystic, who has lived this life in India for more than twenty-five years.[3] Many Indian Christians believe that the ashram type of prayer life, the result of long experience, may be a model for religious communities of the future in the West. Since Western Christians who have experienced it in India are now founding ashrams here and there in the United States, it is well to consider the fundamentals of this type of life of prayer.

1. A Christian ashram is above all a place of prayer conceived according to the Indian tradition as a place to experience God in the inner depths of our own being. In a spirit of peace, calm, and quiet, the ashram offers us the opportunity to be alone with God.

2. The ashram is also a place of awareness, of "active inactivity," of openness to the Spirit who "breathes where he will."

3. The ashram differs from the common conception of the monastery of the past in that it is a place open to others. It is not an enclosure for keeping people out, but rather a center for communion with God to which we are naturally drawn.

4. The ashram is less rigidly structured than the traditional monastery or religious house in order to allow freedom and openness to the movement of the Spirit within us. The goal is not so much

a well-ordered, disciplined life of prayer as it is the creation of an atmosphere of prayer in which each of us is free to respond to the Spirit in his or her own way.

5. The center of life in the ashram is personal prayer, meditation, and contemplation rather than liturgy, which has a central place in traditional monasteries. Ordinarily, the Indian tradition of two hours of meditation at dawn and sunset is followed. In personal prayer, all of us in the ashram seek to discover *our own center* and to experience God in the ground of our being beyond images and thoughts.

6. Liturgical prayer, while subordinate to personal prayer in the ashram, becomes the *corporate* expression of awareness of the presence of God, the sacrament of our communion with God and with one another. This prayer is less structured and more free than traditional liturgical prayer. In order to avoid the danger of the liturgy's becoming a formal routine, our words and gestures are oriented toward contemplation. Short common prayer may be practiced three times a day with the aim of making the psalms a form of meditation. Bible readings are used with pauses for silent prayer after each reading.

7. Great freedom of the forms of prayer and openness to experimentation are practiced in the ashram. Hymns, songs, *namjapa*, and *bhajans* allow for freedom in new types of prayer.

8. Fluidity is practiced in the structures of community life. Attachment to the guru, who has experienced God, may be the only uniting bond of the members. People of either sex may live in the ashram. They may remain a few weeks or months or years without obligation to stay longer. Stability is maintained by a few persons who may form the nucleus of community and who remain for life. But even these may at times go on pilgrimages, live in other ashrams, or retreat to solitude.

9. Social responsibility is linked to the search for God. To realize God, we must also serve God in our neighbors. Thus the ashram is open to people of the neighborhood, especially the poor and needy. But commitment to service which detracts from the central contemplative character of the ashram is avoided.

10. To sum up, the bond of unity in the ashram is neither a place nor a community. Nor is it liturgical prayer or social action. It is the common personal search for the experience of God, for "the knowledge and love of Christ which surpasses all knowledge."

NOTES

1. John Moffitt, *Journey to Gorakhpur*, London, Sheldon Press, pp. 50–57.

2. Abhishiktananda, *Towards the Renewal of the Indian Church*, Ernakulam, Cochin, K.C.M. Press, 1970, pp. 69–75.

3. Bede Griffiths, "Prayer in Christian Ashram," *Praying Seminar*, 217–21.

SUGGESTED READINGS

Abhishiktananda. *Guru and Disciple*. London: SPCK, 1974.

Dwyer, William. "The Theologian in the Ashram," pp. 92–101, in Jean-Pierre Jossua and Johann Baptist Metz, eds., *Doing Theology in New Places*. New York: Seabury Press, 1979.

Griffiths, Bede. *Christian Ashram*. London: Darton, Longman, and Todd, 1966.

Griffiths, Bede. "Kurisumala Ashram," *Eastern Churches Quarterly*, XVI (1964), 226–31.

Rogers, C. Murray. "Hindu Ashram Heritage: The Gift of God," in Christian Duquoc, ed., *Spirituality in Church and World*. New York: Paulist Press, 1965.

Swami Parama Arubi Anandam: A Memorial. Saccidananda Ashram, Tamil Nadu, India, 1959.

Two

EASTERN PRACTICES OF PERSONAL AND GROUP PRAYER FOR CHRISTIANS

Prayer of the Name: Namjapa

General Significance of Prayer of the Name

Namjapa, or Prayer of the Name, is of ancient origin. Whether practiced by Hindus or by Christians, it means the repetition of the name of God over and over again. An old story illustrates the significance of continual repetition *(japa)* of the name *(nama)* of the Lord:

A young student went to visit a *sannyasi* who lived deep in a forest near Brindavan in South India. The holy man came out of his hut, sat on a mat, and motioned the young man to sit near him. The student was intuitively aware of the holiness of the older man. He asked the *sannyasi*, "Sir, how did you attain to your present state?" The saint an-

swered simply, *"Namjapa."* He said no more, and the
young man sat in silence. At last, the student bowed before the *sannyasi* and departed, his heart filled with peace.

Many Westerners regard the frequent offering of one and
the same simple prayer as a trifling preoccupation of simple
people. They do not know the secret through which repetition
of a *mantra,* or name of God, can become a part of our interior
life, a spiritual delight bringing continual joy and nourishment
to our souls, and leading us finally to communion with the
Spirit.

Nama is no mere conventional designation in prayer. A
proper name has a mysterious identity with the person.[1] A
name actually stands for the person it refers to. It often expresses the nature or function of the person, as in Yahweh and
Emmanuel. Change of name often indicates a change of function, as in Abraham, Jacob and Peter. Jesus himself makes
known the name of his Father and asks his disciples to glorify
this name. Also, the Father gave Jesus "a name above all other
names." The apostles proclaim the name of Jesus, and heal the
sick, work miracles, and cast out demons in his name. The
name of the Lord is powerful because it has identity with the
Lord himself.

Even in ordinary human relations, the name stands for the
person much more than the home, the profession, or other
identifications. The answer to the question "Who are you?" is
the name of the person. A name without the person it represents is only an empty sound. It exists only insofar as it establishes a relationship with the person. Thus Christian Swami
Abhishiktananda calls the name "the supreme mental icon."[2]
And Hindu scholar, T.M.P. Mahadevan, declares that name
is superior to and more subtle than form: name signifies
psychic characteristics, while form refers to physical features.
Like an icon, the name participates somehow in the reality of

the person himself. The force of the name is the power of the person himself. Thus the ancient Israelites did not dare to utter the name of Yahweh because of its awesome power. The name of Yahweh was for them non-existent apart from Yahweh himself.

Namjapa, then, means the repetition of a short spiritual invocation or *mantra*. The effects of repetition on our consciousness are of different kinds. Mechanical repetition is, of course, meaningless. But if our mind attends, the repetitive stimulus calms and quiets us. Our minds are emptied of distractions. Rhythmic repetition is also used in some forms of Buddhist meditation like *Zen* and *Satipattana*. Repetition keeps constantly before our minds the thought, action, or emotion expressed in the repeated words. Coupled with memory, it can lead us to concentration in meditation. Moreover, it can create a "subconscious field" in which we live and operate. We can concentrate on a repeated prayer while walking, driving, or carrying out other activities. Prayerful concentration of this type can lead us to almost constant attention to the Divine.

Repetition itself can exist on various levels. Physical repetition can be expressed in gestures, sound, and music. If our minds and hearts become calm, physical repetition alone can be a positive aid to prayer. The second level of repetition is simply mental attention in silence. While a religious image may help to focus our attention, the process does not go beyond the mental. The third level is that of the heart, or center of being, which involves the whole person. Our lips and minds are silent, our hearts are aware, and progressive interiorization is initiated. In the ideal *namjapa*, or Prayer of the Name, all levels of repetition are integrated. It is thus a way to *dhyana* or contemplation. At this stage of prayer, even the name as symbol or icon is transcended. Our souls are simply aware of the presence of the Lord in contemplation.

Hindu Prayer of the Name

The Hindu has always recognized that no short-cut to the Spirit exists. Yet the *Namjapa* has been understood for centuries in Indian tradition as well as in the Christian East as a simple but powerful path to the Lord. The Hindu *namjapa* consists in repeating continually the name of the Lord, either by itself or in a formula of praise. The devotee may repeat the *mantra*, "Rama, Rama," or "Hare Krishna," or some other name of the Lord. He may use beads resembling a rosary, or he may assign a definite period of the day in which he repeats God's name. He continues the repetition while working or walking about, until eventually the prayer repeats itself in his unconscious.

Often the *mantra* is a special prayer assigned to the disciple by the guru as fitting to the person's spiritual aspirations. In the cosmic tradition of India, the ancient *namjapas* were created by sages and mystics through their deep experience of the Spirit. They chanted to the Lord as *Shiva*, the benevolent one, or *Rama*, the lovely one. *Shiva* was said to save those who uttered his name with devotion, even though they were wicked men or murderers. In the *Bhagavatam* we read: "Knowingly or unknowingly, the chanting of the supremely praiseworthy Name burns away man's sins, even as fire reduces fuel to ashes."

The *namjapa* is practiced almost universally in India today. The name itself is considered identical with God, and therefore it is believed to liberate men and women. The orientation of the mantra is toward "one-pointedness," or simplicity of the soul longing for God alone. The prayer thus becomes a central part of a person's life, "a constant humming of the heart to God." By unceasing repetition it is believed to open up an inner dimension below one's surface consciousness.[3] The person who prays deals with words no longer, but becomes aware of the one Word, the Lord who is the living relationship of all men and women with Absolute Reality.

The spiritual value of the Prayer of the Name, therefore, depends not on the particular name or formula chosen but upon the intimate union with God of which it becomes the expression. Though such union may not yet be achieved, the prayer is considered to be powerful in creating the dispositions necessary for union with the Spirit. It can lead desire, emotion, and thought to enriched spiritual understanding. It can give profound meaning to every action of the day, for a person can take God's name anywhere and repeat it anywhere. Eventually, he or she will transcend both sound and the silence of the Name and realize God himself. Yet the *sannyasi* insists that, in order to avoid all temptation to attribute any automatic efficacy to the *namjapa*, the person who prays must recall always the need for moral preparation for contemplation stated in the Eight-Fold Path of Yoga: "He attains the true Name whose words are pure, and who is free from pride and conceit." The *Namjapa* is a *sadhana* for a lifetime search for pure contemplation of God.

Christian Prayer of the Name: The Jesus Prayer

Namjapa in the Christian tradition of Russia and the Near East is the Jesus Prayer.[4] This prayer is always a short appeal to God, repeated continually, to fix the mind on the Lord and offer him praise and love. It may be a simple utterance of the name of the Lord or a prayer formula. The most common Christian mantra is "Lord Jesus, Son of the living God, have mercy on me, a sinner." Others are: "Holy, holy, holy is the Lord," or the Psalm prayer, "Be pleased, O Lord, to deliver me; O Lord, make haste to help me," or the opening words of the Miserere, "Have mercy on me, O Lord." In the Christian, as well as in the Hindu tradition, a person may choose his own brief prayer or receive one from a spiritual director. The Christian Prayer of the Name derives ultimately from the monks of Egypt. St. John Climacus speaks of it in his classic spiritual work, *Scale of Perfection*. In later centuries it spread more and more widely among the Orthodox Churches, especially in Russia, the source of the classic *Way of the Pilgrim*, which made the Prayer of the Name an international spiritual practice.[5]

The beautiful story of *Way of the Pilgrim* is universal in its human appeal. A simple Russian pilgrim wanders from country to country, from spiritual master to spiritual master, seeking only one goal. He has read St. Paul's admonition to "pray always," but no matter how he tries, he cannot achieve his desire. One after the other, each spiritual leader disappoints him. But he will not give up. Finally, the peasant encounters the one great teacher who tells him how to pray always: he must repeat the Name of the Lord continually until finally it becomes so much a part of him that it repeats itself always in his interior self. Then words will be no longer necessary, for he will be one with Jesus forever.

The Prayer of the Name possesses incomparable spiritual and psychological value for the Christian, not merely on the practical level of avoidance of distractions in prayer. The name is like an icon. Icons possess something of the reality they represent. Misused, they could become idols. Properly used, they can lead to a glimpse of the glory of the Lord. The names of Yahweh in the Old Testament and of Jesus in the Gospel are the supreme Christian *namjapas*. The name of God is believed to contain within itself the whole divine mystery, just as a tiny pearl is worth millions in gold. The Lord's name "means all that theologians try to develop in countless volumes." Not conceptualized, it satisfies the longing of men and women for the living water of the woman at the well. Thus, of all mantras or prayers, the name of God is the most powerful. It concentrates the mind and arouses psychic and spiritual energy in a unique way. It is the very power of the Holy Spirit because it is through the Spirit alone that we can speak the name of Jesus, the Lord. The author of *The Cloud of Unknowing* tells us to "fix one word fast to our hearts." This one word is the only Word, the Word of God.

The Jesus Prayer of the Eastern Christian tradition is being revived almost everywhere among Christians today. This *Hesychastic* prayer of the ancient Greek Orthodox Church, while originally a different tradition from the Jesus prayer, later became related closely to the Prayer of the Name.[6] It integrated into itself the ancient prayer formula known as the Jesus Prayer. "Hesychasm" comes from the Greek root "hesychic," meaning quietness. Its method, which goes back to St. John Chrysostom in the fourth century, consists of the repetition of the prayer, "Jesus Christ, Son of God, have mercy on me." The *Philokalia*, a collection of the writings of the Greek fathers over eleven centuries, considered next only to the Bible in the Greek Church, describes the practice of the Jesus Prayer, distinguishing between two methods: voluntary and involuntary.[7] When the prayer becomes so much a part of one that it "prays itself," it corresponds with the "infused prayer" of St. Teresa of Avila, in which the mind becomes still. This type of prayer is pure prayer or prayer of the heart, a gift of grace. St. John Chrysostom writes:

> It is possible to pray at all times, in all circumstances, and
> in every place, to rise from frequent vocal prayer to prayer
> of the mind, and from that to prayer of the heart, which
> opens up the Kingdom of God within us.[8]

Thus "Hesychasm" has been called "a spiritual system of contemplative orientation which finds man's perfection in union with God through continual prayer." It is achieved through silence, tranquility, and peace. Hesychasm is both a prerequisite for contemplation and contemplation itself. It becomes a way of life, as normal as breathing. Through encounter with Christ in the heart, it transforms the person. Neither is there salvation in any other, "for there is no other name under heaven given among men whereby we may be saved" (Acts 4:12). So highly esteemed was the Prayer of the Name in Orthodox tradition, especially in its primitive form, *Kyrie Eleison*, that some Christians substituted it for the Divine Office.

While the Jesus Prayer may become a foretaste of the final stage of union with God, it nevertheless offers help to the beginner in Christian life: it is short, is repeated frequently, addresses Jesus under various titles, begs mercy for the sinner who prays, and is a loving secret movement of the heart. Above all, it can lead to an interior life of communion with the Spirit when pursued faithfully. The author of *The Way of the Pilgrim* writes:

> The prayer of my heart gave me such consolation that I felt there was no happier person on earth than I, and I doubted if there could be greater and fuller happiness in the Kingdom of heaven. Not only did I feel this in my own soul, but the whole outside world also seemed to me to be full of charm and delight. . . . I found in all [persons and things] the magic of the name of Jesus. . . .

The person who establishes his life in the Prayer of the Name, it is written, eventually cannot live without it. For the Christian, the name of Jesus is the only way to the Father. "Abba, Father" is the prayer of Jesus himself. Joining Jesus in calling upon the Father in the power of the Spirit, the Christian participates in the life of the Trinity. The *namjapa* comes to all men and women, whether of East or West, only through the

Spirit. "No one can say 'Jesus is Lord' except by the Holy Spirit" (I Cor 23:3).

Stages of the Prayer of the Name

The Prayer of the Name is of different kinds and degrees.[9] It may be uttered by the lips, or in the mind, or in the heart. No one of these excludes the others. The stages of prayer indicate the depth at which the person is aware of the Divine Presence.

1. *The first stage* is to pray with the lips, to repeat the name of the Lord or the chosen prayer form audibly. Our minds may be distracted; our hearts may be attracted to desires inconsistent with the prayer spoken by our tongues. It does not matter. We must only repeat the Lord's name with respect, despite all distractions, and seek with real longing for the grace of God.

2. In *the second stage*, our lips remain closed. The prayer is whispered in our minds. We give thoughtful attention to the name of the Lord which we repeat. This attention is not so much mental consideration as simple awareness of the name. At this stage, keeping an image of the Lord in mind may be helpful.

3. In *the third stage*, the name of the Lord is placed in our hearts. There is no longer a movement of the lips or even a movement of the mind. The prayer is now in the center of our being. Our minds are quiet. All our desires have passed into the one desire for the Lord, the desire to be one with him and contemplate his glory. Our whole being—body, senses, mind, soul—becomes one in prayer. The real place of encounter with God is the center of our being, symbolized by the heart. In India, this center is called the *guha*, or cave, the "abode of Brahman."

Western Christians sometimes misunderstand the *namjapa* because they confuse it with the recitation of "invocations" they learned in childhood. They do not comprehend the second and third stages of the prayer described above. So long as we are occupied with mental processes, we are not meditating in the Eastern sense. While we remain on the level of the mind only, we run the risk of never entering into the Prayer of the Name in a spiritual sense. We may never become absorbed in awareness of the Holy Spirit within us. Once stabilized in the third stage of the Prayer of the Name, our minds plunge spontaneously to the center of being. We seek the mystery beyond all forms and concepts. Then true prayer is attained. "The only real prayer is the one in which we are no longer aware that we are praying." Thus saints tell us that the Prayer of the Name is the best way to enter into true meditation. Even when we are preoccupied with our daily work, this prayer of the heart can be a kind of atmosphere in which we live. For some people, it becomes so central a part of their lives that they "hear" it through all that they do. They become one with Christ at all times.

Practice of Prayer of the Name

1. While *Namjapa* can be practiced everywhere and always, most spiritual writers agree that the Prayer of the Name requires at least some brief period of time each day devoted to the prayer alone to the exclusion of all other activity.

2. Sit in a quiet, secluded place. Take an easy, restful posture of repose and recollection. Put all thoughts aside. Be aware of your regular breathing.

3. Repeat the prayer you have chosen as you breathe in and breathe out, or as you breathe out only. Move your lips gently until you are ready to repeat the prayer in your mind alone.

4. In the first stages of prayer, the use of a rosary may be effective to maintain attention.

5. Be calm, patient, and repeat the process frequently. Rhythm, repetition, and attention are basic and essential. You may link your prayer to the rhythm of your heart or, if you prefer it, to the rhythm of breathing. Prayer linked to either the heartbeat or breathing may become so continuous that it continues even in sleep.

6. You can pray everywhere, following the exhortation of St. Paul, "Pray always." Keep in mind the admonition of a monk of the Eastern Church: "A common mistake of beginners is to wish to associate the prayer of the Holy Name with inner intensity or emotion. Strenuous exertion is of no avail. As you repeat the name of Jesus, gather your thoughts and feelings around the name quietly, little by little. Gather your whole being around it. Let the name penetrate your soul as a drop of oil spreads and impregnates a cloth. Surrender your whole self and enclose it within the Name of the Lord."

The author of *Way of the Pilgrim* tells us that the Jesus Prayer and the Gospels are one, for the divine Name of Jesus holds in itself the whole Gospel truth. "The Prayer of Jesus is a summary of the Gospels."

The Westerner is amazed, once again, not at the fact that the Jesus Prayer originated in the Eastern Church, but that the *namjapa* of the Hindu presented the same method of prayer long before the birth of Jesus. Surely the religion followed by approximately one out of every eight persons in the world will eventually be one with Christianity, provided that Christians are willing to recognize the preparation for the coming of Christ which appeared centuries ago among their Eastern brothers and sisters.

NOTES

1. Michael Amaladoss, "Namjapa," *Praying Seminar*, pp. 285–96.

2. Abhishiktananda, *Prayer*, pp. 57–64.

3. Vandana, "Indian Spirituality," *Indian Spirituality in Action*, pp. 26–27.

4. Abhishiktananda, *Towards the Renewal of the Indian Church*, pp. 36–40.

5. *Way of the Pilgrim*, trs. from the Russian by R.M. French, London, SPCK, 1963.

6. James Aerthayil, "The Hesychast Method of Prayer," *Dharma*, II (1977), 204–16.

7. Swami Bhajavananda, "Hindu Upasana Vis-à-Vis Christian Meditation," *Dharma*, II (1977), 224–30.

8. Quoted in *The Pilgrim Continues the Way*, London, SPCK, 1941, p. 78.

9. Abhishiktananda, *Prayer*, pp. 59–60.

SUGGESTED READINGS

Bhajanananda, Swami. "Hindu Upasana Vis-à-Vis Christian Meditation," *Dharma*, II (1977), 224–30.

Borchert, Bruno. "The Jesus Movement," pp. 104–08, in Christian Duquoc and Claude Geffré, eds. *The Prayer Life*. New York: Herder and Herder, 1972.

Chethimattam, John B. "Meditation: A Discriminating Realization," *Dharma*, II (1977), 164–72.

Maloney, George. *Centering in the Lord.* Wilmington, Delaware: Michael Glazier, Inc., 1982.

Maloney, George. *Prayer of the Heart.* Notre Dame, Indiana: Ave Maria Press, 1980.

Prayer in Music and Song: Bhajan

Among Hindus, the term *namopasana* describes both the Prayer of the Name, or *namjapa*, and a second type of prayer called *bhajan*. In *namjapa*, as we have seen, the words of prayer are few, and are repeated over and over again. In *bhajan*, the words of prayer are set to music and sung in chorus. This type of group singing is common among both Hindus and Christians in India.[1]

St. Paul exhorted the early Christians to "sing thankfully in your hearts to God, with psalms and hymns and spiritual songs" (Col 3:16). The Fathers of the Church encouraged the singing of psalms and canticles. Yet the Christian tradition has at times maintained an ambivalent attitude toward music in worship, making music subordinate to words. Vatican Council II, however, speaks of the "ministerial function" of music, "whether it adds delight to prayer, fosters unity of minds, or confers greater solemnity upon the sacred rites." Music, then, is a powerful aid to prayer. It creates an atmosphere of joy, celebration, or solemnity. It adds depth and richness to man's faith-response to God. It adds an aesthetic and creative dimension to the more "ordinary" means of prayer, making them more human and experiential.

The emphasis of the Indian *bhajan* is upon prayer and worship in song. Words and music form a harmonious unity. Both are means of creative expression, and each in its own way contributes to the total effect of prayer. There is no presumption, as sometimes happens in Western Christian worship, in favor of language. Music does not merely serve the words of prayer; nor are the words a mere support for music. Thus, in the Indian *bhajan*, both elements have specific roles, and song becomes an experience of worship.

The *bhajan* is always sung in a group. It is corporate worship. A soloist-group structure is integral to it. Occasionally, solo singing may also take place. But ordinarily the group is emphasized through particular care given to the choice of text and melody.

Music in the Indian tradition is an important element in *sadhana*, or spiritual effort toward liberation. Indeed, music is the primordial art and all arts can be reduced to it. The musical sound OM is considered to be the highest and purest experience of the Absolute in sound-symbol. Music as a "way to God" has always been pursued seriously by religious people in India:

> . . . they who are proficient in sound, in the mystic syllable OM, and the music notes which are the form of the Lord Himself, are liberated souls. (Tyagaraja)

The reason why music is a "path to God" is clear in Indian tradition:

> By the knowledge of music, one attains to a state of ab-
> sorption; by attaining such a state, oneness with Shiva the
> Lord can be obtained . . .*(Skanda Purana)*

The efficacy of music, however, is no more automatic than the
efficacy of words in prayer. Music of itself is no more a medium of grace than mere mechanical repetition of the name of
the Lord is true *namjapa*.

Yet music as a medium of spiritual expression and symbolism can be powerful. Music is linked with mood and emotional experience. The aesthetic experience of music can
liberate man, giving him a sense of unity and integration. The
rhythmic aspect of music is essential to its integrating power.
Measure, pattern, regularity, and repetition speak to both
body and spirit. Through the rhythmic aspect of the song, the
whole person is involved. As in the case of repetition of words
in the *namjapa*, a regularly repeated stimulus in music can also
be a powerful aid to concentration in prayer: it can prevent distractions and promote attention to one image or thought to the
exclusion of others. And just as techniques of concentration in
Yoga, *Zen*, and *Satipattana* are based on rhythm, so the
rhythmic element is a unifying factor in the *bhajan*.

The text, as well as the music, of the *bhajan* has its own
role to play. It clarifies the theme as praise, petition, offering,
or adoration. Its repetition deepens mood and heightens consciousness. Continued attention to the Word, as in the practice
of the *namjapa*, deepens the spiritual response of the singer. Attention is also sustained by variety in text, by melodic structure, or by the speed of the music. The linguistic medium
clarifies the dominant *rasa*, or mood, attached to the *raga*,
which is a melodic pattern or mode in Indian music.

Practice of the Bhajan as Prayer

The following suggested practice of *Bhajan as Prayer* is proposed by Michael Amaladoss, Indian Jesuit who writes perceptively of Indian religious art and music.[2] The deeply spiritual experience of listening to a *bhajan* performed by Hindus or by Indian Christians is unforgettable. Yet the writer has also heard beautiful and creative *bhajans* directed by Western singers. *Bhajan* as prayer is profound in its simplicity.

1. The *bhajan* actualizes in song the relationship of the singing group with God.

2. The structure of the *bhajan* should be simple and catching in both words and music. A group should be able to repeat it without previous practice.

3. The rhythm should be clear, marked by a *tala* instrument or by handclapping, thus maintaining the original rhythmic pattern of the Indian *raga*.

4. As the *bhajan* begins, the leader may adopt a theme and make variations on it. The group repeats the theme and its variations.

5. The leader may vary his or her part of the *bhajan*, either the words or the melody, while the group repeats the same phrases, in the structure of a litany.

6. Variations in tempo, either progressive or periodic, are achieved by either speeding up or slowing down.

7. Variety may also be achieved by alternating a song by a soloist or by a small group with the *bhajan* sung by the entire group. For example, the group may take up the main theme of a preceding

song, set in the same *raga* so as not to break the mood. Also, rhythmic variations may be used.

8. A common Indian pattern for the Hindu *bhajan* is the following: a recognized order of spiritual songs composed by different saints from different Indian linguistic regions is introduced; a short invocation is addressed to each saint before his composition is sung; a variety of improvisations follows.

9. The Christian *bhajan*, inspired by the Hindu, can offer a variety of forms. The simplest pattern is to bring the prayer group together, asking each person to propose a song according to the inspiration of the Spirit at the moment. This type of *bhajan* is called *free-style*. In a multi-lingual group, the songs will of course be in different languages. A program may also be organized around a theme, such as praise and thanksgiving, or around a liturgical season, like Advent, Lent, or Easter. It may also take a historical form, for example, the mysteries of the life of Christ, or the interventions of God in history.

10. Since the *bhajan* is worship of God in song, it is better not to interrupt it with readings, spoken reflections, or periods of silence. These may impede the natural movement or dynamic of a worship service in song. A *bhajan* type of hymn, however, may become an element in other forms of prayer, such as a Bible service or morning and evening prayer.

11. Prayer through dance may be a normal culmination of a *bhajan*. Since it involves the whole person, simple gestures and movements of the body may add a further dimension of expression to the medium of song. Also, typical Indian gestures like the throwing of flowers or the rhythmic waving of lighted candles may be used as beautiful symbols. "He who sings melodies in prayer to God is a liberated soul here and now." Let the Western Christian also offer his own creative gestures and songs in prayer.

NOTES

1. Bhajanananda, "Hindu Upasana," *Dharma*, II (1977), pp. 224–25.

2. Michael Amaladoss, "Initiation to Bhajan," *Praying Seminar*, pp. 279–84.

III

Prayer at Daybreak: Samdhya

Samdhya refers to prayers offered by Hindus at the three divisions of the day: morning, noon, and evening. Literally, the word *samdhya* means "union" or "meeting point." Morning is the meeting point of night and day; high noon is the center of the day; evening twilight is the meeting of day and night. Thus the ancient *rishis*, or holy men, prayed three times each day.

Today Hindus often pause at sunrise, at noon, and at twilight, wherever they may find themselves, to beg to be led from darkness to the light of God's glory. *Samdhya* services consist in sipping water, symbolic of purification, while repeating selected mantras and prayers. Meditation may follow.

Water is a universal religious symbol. Sipping water is a common ritual in worship among Easterners. In the *Bhagavadgita*, Krishna tells Arjuna that the person who offers him

148

"even a little water" is dear to him. Bathing in the sacred waters of the Ganges is believed to remove all guilt adhering to evil committed. And the Chinese mystic Lao Tzu included the following among his wise sayings:

> Of the weak things in the world, none is weaker than water. But in overcoming what is firm and strong, nothing can equal it. The soft conquers the hard. Rigidity and hardness are companions of death. Softness and tenderness are companions of life.

Blessing with water was a religious custom long before the Christian era.

The symbolism of light, however, is perhaps most highly emphasized in *samdhya*. The times of *samdhya*—morning, noon and evening—are all associated with the coming or going of the light of the sun. Also, Hindus reverence even the hot sun of summer. They believe that it purifies the elements of earth, water, and air as well as the minds and bodies of men and women. The "angry sun" of May and June cleanses the earth in preparation for the seasons of creation and harvest. To be sure, symbolisms of fire and light are found in every great religion on earth. Yet they are perhaps more central to Hinduism than to any other religion. The most common mantra on the lips of children in India is "From darkness lead us to light."

Without mixing metaphors, we may say that the changes evident at the three divisions of the day—morning, high noon, and twilight—symbolize the rapid changes possible in the life of the man or woman who truly seeks God. Indians have a saying that the fly alights anywhere, but the bee seeks only honey. As we progress in spiritual life, we can see an ocean of goodness even in one drop of the honey of life found in another person— not because we are romantically optimistic, but because we can see the possibility of the person's future growth and emphasize it. We see not what the person is but what he or she can be. "Heaps of cotton can be burned with one match; one gracious glance from God can wipe out mountains of sins. The man who appears as a sinner today may be a saint tomorrow."

Practice of Samdhya as Group Prayer

The following prayer service is planned for a gathering of Hindus and Christians. It will become evident at once that the readings and hymns suggested are deeply meaningful for both Hindu and Christian. Readings from the *Upanishads* and the Bible will lead naturally to quiet meditation. The prayer service below is a morning prayer. Participants may desire to plan similar group prayers for noonday and evening worship.

A Hindu-Christian Morning Prayer: Darkness to Light

1. *Introduction to the Prayer Service, by Leader*

2. *Opening Hymn—Darkness Has Faded (Christian Prayer, No. 5)*
    or
    Morning Has Broken (Christian Prayer, No. 4)

3. *Opening Prayers*

Hindu:

From non-being lead us to being;
From darkness lead us to light;
From death lead us to immortality.

That selfsame light which shines
Throughout all things,
Throughout the universe,
Throughout the worlds
Beyond which there is nothing further,
Is also the light which shines
Within the heart of man.

(*Brihadaranyaka* and *Chandogya Upanishads*)

Christian:

The Father has made us worthy to join the saints
And with them to inherit the light.
He has taken us out of the power of darkness
And created a place for us in the kingdom
Of the Son that he loves,
And in him we gain our freedom.

(Col 1:12–14)

4. *Brief Meditation on the Readings*

5. *Mantra*

Hindu:

Let us meditate on the most excellent
Light of the Creator God
And let him inspire our intellect.

Christian:

God of God, Light of Light,
True God of True God,
Receive our prayer.

6. *Brief Meditation on the Mantras*

7. *Chant*

Hindu:

Inner Light, outer Light,
Inward Light, greater than the great,
Light of Light, self-existent Light,
Auspicious one, greater than the great,
Hear us.

Christian:

We, with our unveiled faces
Reflecting like mirrors the brightness of the Lord,
All grow brighter and brighter
As we are turned into the image that we reflect;
This is the work of the Lord
Who is Spirit.
It is the same God that said,
"Let there be light shining out of darkness,"
Who has shone in our minds to radiate
The light of the knowledge of God's glory,
The glory of the face of Christ.

(2 Cor 3:18; 4:6)

8. *Longer Meditation on the Readings*

9. *Closing Prayer*

Hindu:

Let there be peace in the sky,
Peace in the mid-regions, on the earth,
Peace in water and plants,
Peace among all the powers of the world,
Peace among all men and women in the world,

Peace of Brahma among all.
Shanti.
May this peace be with you, with me.
OM, Peace, Peace, Peace.

Christian:

The city did not need
The sun or the moon for light,
Since it was lit by the radiant glory of God
And the lamb was a lighted torch for it.
The nations will live by its light. . . .
The gates will never be shut by day—
And there will be no night there. . . .

(Rev 21:23–25)

10. *Closing Hymn*

O God of Light (*Christian Prayer*, No. 15)
        or
Lead, Kindly Light

I V

Prayer for Light:
Deepavali

Throughout history the great religions of the world have always regarded light as a symbol of Divinity. Particularly in the East, people have gathered annually in family or in community to light lamps or candles and enkindle their hearts with devotion and joy. Their prayers are petitions for spiritual light as well as for peace and harmony among all men and women.

In the north of India, the Hindu Festival of Lights is called *Deepavali;* in the south, *Kaarthikai Deepam.* It is celebrated on the new moon day in September-October in the north, and on the full moon day in October-November in the south.

Attending a Festival of Lights celebration in India for the first time, the writer asked a participant to explain the significance of *Deepavali*. In typical Hindu fashion, the reply was a legendary story:

A disciple asked his guru, "Sir, how can I find the true Light?"

"Come along," said the guru. "I will show you."

The teacher then took his follower to a lake, where both plunged into the water. Suddenly the guru reached over and pushed the disciple's head under water. A few moments later he released him and asked: "Well, how did you feel?"

"Oh, I was dying for a breath of air," gasped the follower.

Then the guru said: "When you desire God with the same intensity as that, you will find the true Light!"

During the early centuries when artificial lighting was extremely limited, people in India came together by the light of the moon to partake of food together, to unite with family and friends, and to perform marriages. Moonlight was a special gift of God. But all these activities were by-products overshadowed by the dominant religious purpose of the festival: to seek divine light from the Lord. Various pilgrimage centers, like Calcutta in the north and Madras in the south, developed over the years. People traveled on foot or on carts and rickshaws to participate in community and family celebrations. The festivity aspect of the celebration, often accompanied by colorful and dramatic religious presentations, was strong.

Hindus believe that men and women proceed in their realization of God from the gross to the subtle, from purgation to ultimate divine union. The Festival of Lights symbolizes entry from darkness to light in the illuminative way to God. In south India, Lord Shiva is worshiped in his role of eternal guru, meaning one who dispels darkness and guides men and women to the unitive way in the spiritual life.

In order to advance from darkness to light, it is essential to seek the Lord in all simplicity without pretense. An age-old Hindu warning states: "Beware of these five: the man who wears a jewel in his ear, one who is secretive and does not talk at all, one who cannot keep a secret and talks too much, a woman with a double veil, and the water of a pond which is covered with scum." In short, a person must know who he or she is, and appear before God and human beings without barriers to true identity.

The artlessness of the ancient Festival of Lights continues in celebrations throughout India today. Though some festivals are more sophisticated than in times gone by, the central emphasis on the significance of divine light remains unchanged.

Practice of Inter-Faith Festival of Lights

The following service is based on an ecumenical religious celebration in Tamil Nadu, south India, of Hindus, Christians, and Muslims. The service can be followed, with or without change, for community prayer of members of various Western Christian and non-Christian groups.

1. *Introduction*

Leader:

As we gather together to celebrate a Festival of Lights, let us pray that our burning lamps (or candles) may fill our homes and our communities with the brightness of the peace and harmony of the Lord.

2. *Invocation*

All:

From the unreal lead us to the real,
From darkness lead us to light,
From death lead us to immortality.

3. *Lighting of Lamps or Candles*

This part of the ceremony may be accompanied by an interpretative dance.

4. *First Reading*

Brilliant is the light of lights
Which knowers of the self know;
He, the one light giving heat
With thousands of rays,
Is the Lord of Lights.
Infinite King, I see thee lighting
Earth, heaven, and hell,
Turning darkness into dazzling day.
Hail, highest majesty!
My soul dissolves
When I behold your burning glances.

(*Prasna Upanishad* and *Bhagavadgita*—Adapted)

5. *Improvised Group Song–Bhajan*

6. *Second Reading*

In the beginning God created the heavens and the earth.
Now the earth was a formless void,
There was darkness over the deep,
And God's spirit hovered over the water.
God said, "Let there be light,"
And there was light.

(Gen 1:1–3)

God is light; there is no darkness in him at all.
If we say that we are in union with God
While we are living in darkness,

We are lying because we are not living the truth.
But if we live our lives in the light,
As he is in the light,
We are in union with one another. . . .

(1 John 1:5–7)

When Jesus spoke to the people again, he said:
"I am the light of the world;
anyone who follows me will not walk in the dark;
he will have the light of life."

(John 8:12)

7. *A Christian Hymn*

I Sing the Mighty Power of God (*Christian Prayer*, No. 10)
or
Splendor of Creation (*Christian Prayer*, No. 130)

8. *Third Reading*

The name of Allah is compassionate, merciful.
The sun shows his mid-day brightness;
The day reveals his splendor;
The night veils him.

Allah is the light of the heavens and the earth.
His light is compared to a niche enshrining a lamp,
The lamp within a crystal of star-like brilliance . . .
Its very oil would shine forth, though no fire touched it.
Light upon light, Allah guides to his light those whom he
    wills . . .
Indeed, the man from whom Allah withholds his light
Shall find no light at all.

(*The Holy Koran*—Adapted)

9. *Silent Prayer*

10. *Recital of prayers by representatives of each religious community for the welfare of all.*

11. *Common Prayer*

All:

Great God of all, bless our country, this land
of varied creeds and cultures, of people speaking
different tongues, of saints and scholars, of rich
and poor, of light and darkness.

O Lord of Light, you are the source of our destiny.
Your name echoes in our hills and valleys, chants
in the waves of the seas. We pray for your
blessing and we sing your praise. Liberate our
land from the darkness of war, corruption,
poverty, misery, provincialism, and ignorance.
Teach us that it is useless to curse the darkness.
Give us your power to overcome the encircling
darkness by lighting the lamps of our lives with
your love and the service of your people.

(*Inter-Faith Dialogue in Tiruchirapalli*, p. 50—Adapted)

12. *Concluding Hymn*

O Worship the King (*Christian Prayer*, No. 43)
or
Creator of the Earth and Skies (*Christian Prayer*, No. 86)

A social gathering concludes the Festival of Lights.

Prayer for All Human Beings: Pongal

Pongal is a Hindu feast of ancient origin celebrated to thank God for the harvest. In India today, Hindus and Christians join in annual prayers of thanksgiving as the crops are reaped. However, a *Pongal* celebration may be held at any time to pray for the welfare of a community or of all the children of God.

From time immemorial, the earth and its fruitfulness have been considered divine by Hindus as well as by other ancient peoples. Human beings have always been amazed by the inexhaustible fertility of the earth, by its mysterious capacity for receiving decaying life within itself in order to bring life to birth once again in a magnificent burst of freshness and vigor. Ancient people experienced this fertility as a symbol of divine creative power. The Hindus expressed the fruitfulness of the earth thus: "The Earth is a mother; I am the child of Earth. . . . Born of her, mortals return to her."

Certain phenomena of the earth, on the basis of analogy, are experienced by Hindus as revealing particular manifestations of the divine more powerfully than others. These revelations are therefore associated more closely with religious experience. The immense variety of flowers, fruits, grains, and herbs communicates to men and women the infinite creative power of God which brings all creatures to life and sustains them through divine providence.

Grain, for example, symbolizes not only the sacred power of fertility but also belief in the afterlife. Grain is associated with the striking mysterious perpetuity of life itself. Grass is used by Hindus in purification rites, and is held to be a symbol through which health and well-being are implored from the Divine. Unborn children are believed to live symbolically under the grass or the bare earth in springs, fountains, and flowing water. Thus human beings are mysteriously alive not only in the present but also in the past and the future life. Because of the divine power within the earth, newborn children are laid upon the ground to receive the divine presence and power.

The seriously sick and the dying are also laid upon the bare ground, as close to the earth as possible, to obtain the divine intervention symbolized in the earth. Divine protection is thus prayed for at the moment of death. When a person dies, placing the body or the ashes finally in the earth expresses belief in afterlife and reincarnation. Ritual expression of belief in life after death and in rebirth through divine power is symbolized powerfully by the earth itself.

When we turn to the consideration of the sacredness and fruitfulness of the earth as related to Christianity, we immediately think of the resurrection of Christ and the resurrection of all men and women. The symbol of earth can relate to Christ as Savior, to cleansing, to spiritual rebirth, to offering of one-self, to joy in the Lord, to immortal life. Christians are familiar with the many symbolisms of light, water, fire, flowers, and grain. Many creative ways to use these symbols in Christian prayer have been developed, especially since Vatican II.

The fundamental primordial realities of human living—water, wine, bread, oil, roots, trees—have been spiritually meaningful to Christians for hundreds of years. The natural symbolisms of these elements are ennobled by Christians through linking them with Christ and the paschal mystery. Christians can also borrow Eastern symbols to make prayer more meaningful. These symbols can help us to meet with greater confidence and joy in the Lord our common crises in both life and death.

A Hindu–Christian Pongal Service

The following Hindu-Christian Pongal Service is modeled partly on a service attended by both Hindus and Christians at Aikya Alayam ashram in Madras, South India.[1] A discussion by Hindus and Christians of the significance of prayer at harvest time followed the collective prayer.

1. *Introduction*

Leader:

As we come together to thank
God for the harvest, let us bless
his name and pray for the welfare
of all men and women.

2. *Invocation Song*

    All You Nations (1, 2, 3) (*Christian Prayer*, No. 11)

3. *Prayer of Adoration*

Leader:

Glory to You, O Source of all, O All-knowing One.
Glory to you, O Origin of Scriptures, O Pure Lord.

Community:

Glory to You, O Ocean of Eternal Joy.
O Lord of all countries, Glory to You.
You grant us redemption always, Glory to You.
                        (Manikavasagar)

Leader:

You will not turn away from the loving prayers
Of the lowliest of your servants,
For in your realm pride cannot strut,
Humility alone gains benediction.

Community:

With bowed head and folded hands,
Let us sing the story of your greatness.
Speaking your name satisfies our longings,
Remembering your deeds gives us strength.
                          (Tulsidas)

Leader:

Let us chant: How sweet is your name.

Community:

How sweet is your name.

4. *Community Contemplation: Prayer of Devotion*

Leader:

Love the Lord, O my soul, for
A body without eyes,
A shrine without light,
So are you without the Lord.
The Lord alone is your salvation:
Love him with adoration.

Community:

Love the Lord, O my soul, for
A well without water,
A moonless night,
A barren waste without rain,
So are you without the Lord.
The Lord alone is your salvation.
Love him with devotion.

(Nanak)

Leader:

Holding my hand, You lead me,
My companion everywhere.
As I walk, leaning on You,
You bear my burden.

Community:

So like happy children we play
In your dear world, O God,

And everywhere, we say,
Your joy is spread abroad.
                    (Tukaram)

Leader:

Let us chant: Holy, Holy, Holy, Lord God.

Community:

Holy, Holy, Holy, Lord God.

5. *First Reading*

Let the wise one study the Scriptures,
Intent on Wisdom;
But later let him discard them
Like the husk when he wants rice.
            (Amritabindu Upanishad, 18)

6. *Second Reading*

Do not work for food that cannot last,
but work for food that endures to eternal life,
the kind of food the Son of Man is offering you,
for on him the Father, God himself, has set his seal. . . .
It is my Father who gives you the bread from heaven,
the true bread;
for the bread of God
is that which comes down from heaven
and gives life to the world. . . .
I am the bread of life.
He who comes to me will never be hungry;
he who believes in me will never thirst.
                    (John 6:27, 32–33, 35)

7. *Silent Reflection*

8. *Prayer of Petition*

All:

> This is my prayer to thee, my Lord—
> Strike, strike at the penury in my heart.
> Give me the strength
> Lightly to bear my joys and sorrows.
> Give me the strength
> To make my love fruitful in service.
> Give me the strength
> Never to disown the poor
> Or bend my knees before insolent might.
> Give me the strength
> To raise my mind high above trifles.
> And give me the strength
> To surrender my strength to thy will in love.
>
> (Tagore)

9. *Closing Pongal Hymn*

> *For the Fruits of His Creation* (*Christian Prayer*, No. 37)
> or
> *We Plough the Fields and Scatter* (*Christian Prayer*, No. 47)

NOTE

1. See also "Pongal Prayer Service," *Inter-Faith Dialogue in Ti-ruchirapalli*, pp. 51–53.

V I

Prayer of Silence:
Gandhian Maun

It is a common custom of Hindus, both monks and lay people, to set time aside each week for complete silence, prayer, and reflection. A short period each day, or one day each week, is chosen. The "Gandhian Monday" is famous throughout India. No matter what work Gandhi had to accomplish, no matter what important visitor came to see him, he refused to utter a single word on Mondays.

It is interesting that the name of Mahatma Gandhi should be associated with the Prayer of Silence. Gandhi's insistence on truth, non-violence, and human community puts him in the "class" of Indian ethical reformers rather than that of contemplatives or mystics.[1] In other words, his passionate way of service marks his central goal in life as dominantly *karma marga* (path of action) rather than *bhakti* (devotion) or *jnana* (wisdom).

Moral outrage at the plight of the poor and the "disease"

of color prejudice was his motivation in carrying out five great non-violent campaigns against injustice. The aim of his method, called "firmness in truth," was conversion to the right, not coercion. The force he used was moral, not physical. He appealed to the inherent moral instincts of others through his own uncompromising fasting and self-purification. Non-violent disobedience was his strategy. He suffered the oppressor's anger, submitted to arrest, but never surrendered.

Gandhi's unparalleled witness to the call of service to the human community is essential in considering his character. His personal devotion to God and deep concern for religious values are indubitable. Yet in no sense was he an Indian mystic as Ramakrishna and Vivekananda were. When speaking of his "experiments with truth," Gandhi wrote: "They are spiritual, or rather moral; for the essence of religion is morality." Here Gandhi differed with the majority of all saints and mystics, who would have seen morality as the *fruit* of interior union with God.

From the age of thirty-five, Gandhi held daily prayer meetings for his followers. His personal devotion to God was deep. Yet he never found the personal guru whom he felt to be necessary for his spiritual realization. Once he was asked, "Have you realized anything of God, Gandhiji?" His answer was: "I am knocking at the door." At another time, when voting was about to take place on a controversial program of the Indian Congress Working Committee, he remarked to a Ramakrishna monk, "Pray I may not win the vote. Then I will come and lose myself in meditation at your monastery."

As Gandhi's faith matured, he felt a strong urge toward complete spiritual renunciation. Yet his faith in God was not based on an indubitable experience of God. He writes in his autobiography, "I have not seen him, neither have I known him. . . . I have no word for characterizing my belief in God." And later he wrote: "What I want to achieve—what I have been striving and pining to achieve for thirty years—is self-realization, to see God face to face, to attain Moksha [liberation]. I live and move and have my being in pursuit of this goal."

The influences on Gandhi's spirituality were many: the *Bhagavadgita*, the *Mahabharata*, Tolstoy, Thoreau, the Christian Gospel, particularly the Sermon on the Mount. Anyone who studies his life will be convinced that he ultimately integrated his contemplation with his unequaled service of humanity. *Gandhian Maun* is a symbol of how many Western Christians can integrate their own goal of justice and peace through active service with the Eastern path of interior communion with God. For the person who seeks experience of God, the two goals cannot be separated.

Practice of Maun

Christian groups may find it convenient to practice "Maun" on weekends. Though it is the custom of many Western Christians to set aside days of recollection, the dominant characteristic of "Maun" is prayer and meditation in complete silence.

1. The hours or days of *Maun* are chosen by an individual or by a prayer group.

2. Complete silence is maintained in prayer and meditation.

3. Penance, fasting, and abstinence are practiced on the day of *Maun*.

4. The individual or the members of the group have freedom to plan times of prayer, spiritual reading, quiet walking, and reflection, sometimes culminating in a Holy Hour.

5. If a prayer group participates in *Maun*, silence is broken after the Holy Hour to share spiritual reflections among the group.

6. The essential element of *Maun* is reflection. Since spiritual maturity does not always develop from experience but from experience reflected upon, the *Maun* group shares personal reflections after silence.

7. A person who finds it sometimes impossible to set aside hours for *Maun* may practice *Maun* "in spirit" once a week. Interiority may be cultivated even during active employment.

8. People have a right to expect a life of prayer and penance from sincere believers. Therefore the witness value of *Maun* is important, especially for Christians in a non-Christian culture.

NOTE

1. See John Moffitt, *Journey to Gorakhpur*, pp. 216–36.

VII

The Lord's Prayer:
A Hindu Reflection

When Jesus taught us how to pray by giving us the Lord's Prayer, he did not offer us formulas and methods. The Lord's Prayer is not a prescribed statement to be repeated again and again: it is a beautiful description of the spirit in which we approach the Father. We can make it a mechanical exercise, but if we do so we are not praying. The Our Father is the essence of Jesus' own experience and his message to us. If we allow even one phrase of the Lord's Prayer, "Thy will be done," for example, to sink into our hearts, it can lead us to contemplation and peace. We can let this one phrase, like a *namjapa* or Prayer of the Name, become so much a part of us that we pray always.

Just before Jesus gave his disciples the gift of the Lord's Prayer, he let them know that he was not thinking about mere repetition of words: "And when you pray, do not keep on babbling like pagans, for they think they will be heard because of their many words. Do not be like them, for your Father knows what you need before you ask him" (Mt 6:7–8).

In Luke's account of the gift of the Lord's Prayer, Jesus adds the parable of the man who begged bread from his friend at midnight when the latter was sleeping. Finally, the friend granted his request only because of his resolute persistence (Lk 11:5–10). The persistent follower of Jesus prays always. If we ask the Father, we know that we will receive. Jesus emphasizes his teaching with extraordinary power by adding: "Which of you fathers, if your son asks for a fish, will give him a snake instead? Or if he asks for an egg, will give him a scorpion? If you then, though you are evil, know how to give good gifts to your children, how much more will your Father in heaven give the Holy Spirit to those who ask him" (Lk 11:11–13).

Perhaps there is danger of our overlooking, in the above words of Jesus, the crucial significance of the gift to be given to us. In our joy over Jesus' promise that the Father will hear our prayer, we may forget what he tells us to pray for: we are to "ask for the Holy Spirit." When we receive the Holy Spirit, our "babbling words" become meaningless, for we receive the Spirit only in interior silence.

The following reflection is a shortened version of "The Lord's Prayer," which appears in *The Sermon on the Mount According to Vedanta*, by Swami Prabhavananda, a Ramakrishna monk of Madras, India. This meditation is thoroughly Eastern in spirit and mood. It may be well to remember that Jesus himself was an Easterner. In the manner of the East, Jesus speaks in parables. The *sannyasi*, too, tells us two little parables in his reflection on the Our Father. They are the type of story that returns to our consciousness again and again long after our reading. One parable tells of the experience of a beautiful young woman who gave her whole life to seeking interior experience of God and considered her final joy well worth the price. The other presents God as the mother who is always ready to grasp her wayward child in her arms. The concept of God as mother is not uncommon in the East. The Hindu *sannyasi* can perhaps offer us thoughts of the Father that expand our knowledge of him and lead us to him through the Holy Spirit, the mutual love of Father and Son.

The Lord's Prayer: An Eastern Reading

The Lord's Prayer is God-centered prayer. Man-centered prayer beseeches God to enrich life on earth, to remove suffering, to provide comfort, wealth and success. God-centered prayer seeks God alone, knowing that God-realization is the whole purpose of life.

Our Father . . .

Like other great spiritual teachers, Christ taught us to worship God as a personal being. To love the Lord with all our heart, mind, and strength, we must enter into a relationship with him that makes him our own.

We begin with our relationship to God as child to parent. We reverence, trust and love our Father with absolute confidence. He protects us. We are safe with him. Gradually we come to experience that he is more than a Father: he is Absolute, he is all in all.

Who art in heaven . . .

Christ tells us that our Father is in heaven. Heaven has no spatial existence. But the kingdom of heaven is within us. To be in heaven is to be in union with our Father within our own hearts. But earth as well as heaven is within us. As long as we are not purified through prayer and worship, we are conscious of earth. Until we are able to go beyond time and space, we think of God within our hearts and pray to him there. We need not yet seek a heaven beyond.

Hallowed be thy name . . .

God and his name are one. "Glorify the Lord with me, let us praise his name" (Psalms). "Whosoever shall call upon the name of the Lord shall be saved" (Romans). The name of the Lord is the mantra, the sound-symbol of infinite spiritual power. When we hallow the name of God continually, God gradually takes possession of our conscious minds. Then no matter what we say or do or think, we praise him. His name becomes for us light, nourishment, and delight, leading us to union with him.

Thy kingdom come . . .

When a Hindu performs ritualistic worship, his first prayer is: "As with eyes wide open a man sees the sky above him, so the seers see the Supreme Truth, God." When our eyes are opened, we shall see God's kingdom existent here and now. This is not a hope for the future. God's kingdom has already come; it has always been with us. When we pray to our Father, we should forget ourselves, know that he alone exists in himself. Through praying thus, we will actually learn to see his kingdom in our hearts and all around us.

Thy will be done on earth, as it is in heaven . . .

Throughout history, in every country, all sorts of people have done exactly what they wanted to do and claimed that they were doing God's will. Until the day comes that we are in union with God, so that we are filled with the Holy Spirit, we cannot know for certain what his will may be. But even in our ignorance, we can know that the Father's will is whatever will lead us to him. We can ask him to guide us to his will alone.

Give us this day our daily bread . . .

We pray that divine grace, our daily bread, may be granted to us today and forever. An old Hindu parable tells of a beautiful young girl who went into the desert alone to see God. She became a young woman, a middle-aged woman, and finally an old woman. In all that time she had not seen God, but she waited for him eagerly, day after day, year after year, ready for him at every moment of every day. At last God came. He passed by her, she saw him, and her whole life was blessed.

To ask God for daily bread is to know that his grace may be given to us at any moment, and at the same time to be prepared to wait patiently. No one can "buy" God with spiritual practices. Grace is a gift. But we must be ready, prayerful, and watchful. "The breeze of grace is always blowing. Set your sail to catch that breeze."

And forgive us our debts, as we forgive our debtors . . .

A Hindu would read "debts" as the debts of "karma." The word "karma" stands for our actions and their consequences. Our own deeds bring us happiness or misery. We are responsible for our own character and we must hold no one else responsible. If we accept this responsibility for our own acts, then we shall find it easy to forgive those in debt to us. Only when we forgive others in our hearts can we expect forgiveness from God.

We cannot forgive when our sense of ego makes us feel separate from God. The *Upanishads* compare our vast universe to a wheel. Upon it are all creatures subject to birth and death. Round and round it turns and never stops. It is the wheel of God. As long as we consider ourselves separate from God, we revolve upon the wheel in bondage to birth and death. But when through the grace of God we realize our union with God, we revolve upon the wheel no longer. We achieve immortality. To free ourselves from bondage, we must surrender our sense of ego to God, and pray for forgiveness of our debts. Then we can forgive others and reach union with God.

And lead us not into temptation, but deliver us from evil . . .

Fascinated by God's creation, men and women often fail to see that God dwells in their own hearts. Forgetting God, we become slaves to the temptations of God's world, and live in bondage to ignorance and the cravings of our egos. The *Bhagavadgita* describes the process by which we succumb to temptation:

> Thinking about sense-objects will attach you to sense-objects; grow attached, and you become addicted; thwart your addiction, it turns to anger; be angry and you confuse your mind; confuse your mind, you forget the lesson of experience; forget experience, you lose discernment; lose discernment, and you miss life's only purpose.

The *sannyasi* prays that he may not be deluded by the bewitching world.

God does not lead us into temptation, but acts toward us like a mother who watches her child playing with his toys. As long as he is happy with his toys, she lets him play. But when he tires of play and cries for her, she runs to him and takes him in her arms. As long as we are satisfied with the fascinating things of earth, God lets us play. But when we turn from his creation and become restless for him, he graciously reveals himself to us.

For thine is the kingdom, and the power, and the glory, now and forever. Amen.

To escape from fascination with creation and gain our freedom in the spirit, we must restrain our preoccupation with the world and turn within our hearts where the Spirit lives. We must take refuge in God and pray for the gift of divine grace. Then we shall know the meaning of "the kingdom, and the power, and the glory" of God. We shall experience God everywhere, in every object and every creature. "From Joy springs this universe, in Joy exists this universe, and unto Joy goes back this universe." God is Joy.

Glossary

Ahimsa · Not harming or non-injury ranks among the foremost virtues of the Hindu ethical code, expressive of sacredness of all life. It implies living one's life without doing harm—physical, mental, emotional or moral—to anyone. The sin of killing is especially heinous, since blood is the principle of life and is filled with potency. The doctrine of *ahimsa* is often held up as India's great contribution to ethics. Gandhi brought *ahimsa* from the sphere of religion to the sphere of politics.

Arjuna · Prince hero of the epic *Mahabharata* who seeks the advice of Krishna in the solution of his own problem: whether or not he should seek victory in battle by fighting and killing his own people. Krishna's response, in the *Bhagavadgita*, is venerated by many Hindus as the utterance of the Supreme Deity.

Atman · Sanskrit term for the spirit hidden in the human heart, which is one with the universal spirit, *Brahman*.

Banaras or Varanasi · One of the seven holy cities of Hindus, situated on the sacred Ganges. The city is revered as the most sacred spot on earth, the center of *Siva* worship, and the birthplace of all religion. Thousands of Hindus go to *Banaras* to end their days.

Bhagavadgita · "Song of the Lord" is a philosophical poem in dialogue form, comprising eighteen stanzas of the *Mahabharata*. Embodies teachings of *Lord Krishna* given to *Arjuna*. The doctrine of *bhakti*, or loving devotion to the Lord, is the chief glory of the *Gita*.

Bhajan · Worship or prayer in song in which words and music form a harmonious unity, with no presumption in favor of language. The song is an experience and expression of worship.

Bhakti · Fervent devotion to God. In the orthodox view, *bhakti* implies: belief in a personal God of absolute love, mercy, and grace; total submission to the will of God; seeking God as a refuge for complete protection; belief in the divinity of the human soul and God's willingness to save all who love him. The influence of Christianity on the doctrine of *bhakti* has frequently been pointed out.

Brahma · The Creator and the first God of the Hindu triad, of which *Vishnu* the preserver and *Siva* the destroyer are the other two. Brahma is associated in ancient cosmology with the creation of the universe. The wife of *Brahma*, *Sarasvati*, is goddess of wisdom and science, speech and music, and deviser of the Sanskrit script.

Brahmin · The first of the four Hindu castes. The other three are the warrior (king or knightly caste), the merchant (trader, grocer, money-lender), and the menial worker. The outcastes or "untouchables" were beyond the pale of Hindu society. The Brahmins were a priestly caste, although today a Brahmin is not necessarily a priest. The Brahmin conducted rites and sacrifices, and studied and taught the *Vedas*.

Buddha · Indian prophet Siddartha Gautama, called the Buddha, "the Awakened One," who preached a way of enlightenment that he called *dharma*.

Darshan · Seeing a holy person and receiving the blessing derived from seeing him or her. Analogous to the attitude of Roman Catholics when having an audience with the Pope.

Dharma · Righteousness; duty; one of the four goals of human life, the other three being aesthetic enjoyment, economic security, and salvation or liberation from delusion.

Ganges · Sacred river of the Hindus. The water of the Ganges is regarded as an elixir. Taken daily, it was believed to confer immortality. A bath in it purified one from all sin. Confining the body of a deceased person to the river ensured his entry into bliss.

Guru · A spiritual preceptor or leader; one who "leads from darkness into light." The *guru* receives pupils in his *asrama* or hermitage. *Gurus* are needed because inherited wisdom is handed down through inspired leaders. The selection of a proper *guru* is therefore imperative.

Harijan · "Devotee of the Lord." Term applied by Gandhi to the "untouchables" of Hindu society. Gandhi fasted and campaigned to erase the blot of "untouchability" from Hindu society. Ramakrishna and Vivekananda also strongly opposed this injustice.

Hatha Yoga · *Yoga* as physical discipline; has as its goal bodily preparation for meditation. Meditation is *essential* to *yoga*.

Hesychasm · A word of Greek origin meaning "quiet" or "the silent life"; also called the Jesus Prayer tradition.

Jnana · True knowledge; spiritual wisdom, knowing through inner experience or intuitive wisdom that God exists.

Karma · The principle of universal causality resulting from action. One of the basic constituents of the Hindu philosophical system. A term of wide application, *karma* is used to mean action, deeds, destiny, causality, effect. It is rooted in the idea of universal order which is the foundation of *dharma*, or right action. It is based on the premise that there is no random combination of events, no accidental occurrence, since causality underlies all. *Karma* is a cosmic law of punishment and reward for good and evil; a law of moral retribution, eternally recurring. "Man is punished by his sins, not for them." *Karma* is mitigated by *bhakti*, through which surrender to God leads to the bestowal of God's grace.

Krishna · Variously a god, a scholar, a warrior, and a king. As a god, Krishna is the most celebrated deity of the Hindu pantheon, and the eighth incarnation of Vishnu. His life-story, told in the epic *Mahabharata*, is known to every Hindu.

Mandala · A symbolical diagram usually bounded by a circle, within which squares, triangles, and labyrinthine patterns are engraved on metal, stone, wood, paper, or other material. Elaborations within and around the mandala pattern are explained by Hindu philosophers. Also adopted by the Jungian school to symbolize the structure of the deep psyche.

Mantra · Sacred verse from Hindu Scriptures; sacred words composed by sages of extraordinary power and wisdom. The mantra is learned through the living voice of a *guru*. A support for meditation, it transcends all concepts related to the words.

Marga · Path, road, or way leading to *moksha*, or salvation. Commonly added to an operative word: *bhakti, karma, jnana*.

Maya · Illusion; false knowledge; the negative principle, cosmic delusion which leads to error.

Moksha · Salvation or liberation; a prime goal of human life on earth.

OM · Another name for God, the primal word that includes all sounds; the wisdom contained in the Scriptures which has existed always and through which God brings forth the universe. Compared with St. John: "In the beginning was the Word."

Patanjali · Author of the *Yoga Sutras*. Founder of the Raja Yoga system.

Puja · Ceremonial worship; often a simple daily offering of flowers, fruit, or water to the chosen deity.

Raga · Name given to a class of modal melodies which constitute the highest expression of Indian classical music. Each *raga* is believed to create a specific emotional effect that "colors" the mind of the listener.

Ramakrishna · Famous nineteenth century Bengal brahmin who believed that all religions are true. The *Ramakrishna Mission* has more than one hundred centers in all parts of the world.

Ramayana · One of the two great epics of India, the other being the *Mahabharata*. Origin is disputed, as are historical and spiritual interpretations. Considered epic of the soul written in symbolism.

Rishi · A sage, patriarch, poet, or elder possessed of extraordinary power and wisdom. The *rishi* lived in a forest or mountain retreat, called an *ashram*, with his disciples.

Saccidananda · Literally "being–awareness–bliss": the name of the Lord; the goal of perfection.

Sadhana · Quest for perfection; a path or way to God.

Sadhu · A generic term applied to a Hindu ascetic or healer. May be an anchorite living in solitude, or a cenobite living in monastic community.

Samadhi · Union with God; state of deep contemplation or spiritual ecstasy; compared with the "unitive way" of St. John of the Cross.

Sannyasa · The fourth stage of life, or monkhood, the first three being those of the student, the householder, and the recluse. The monk or ascetic who renounces the world is called a *sannyasi*.

Siva · Major god of the Hindu pantheon, forming with *Brahma* and *Vishnu* the great triad of Hindu deities. The director of destinies, death, and destruction. Embodies the mystic forces of the human soul as well as the cosmic forces of nature. As the "Great God," he represents the character of fatality in the life epic of the universe.

Swami · Literally, lord; religious teacher; priest.

Tagore, Rabindranath · Bengali poet who was subject to mystical experiences from the age of seventeen. Believed that Reality is one—*Brahma*, the Absolute—and man is a fragment of the Real. Awarded Nobel Prize for Literature in 1913.

Tukaram · *Marathi* religious writer. His mystical hymns are addressed to Krishna.

Tulsidas · Hindu poet and mystic whose beliefs have been likened to those of Christianity.

Upanishads · Philosophical and meditative portions of the *Vedas*. First consistent expression of a philosophical doctrine in Hinduism, but characterized by intuitive understanding rather than by logical systemization into any scheme of philosophy as such. Extremely subtle, sublime, and profound, with an overwhelming influence on Indian thought. Fundamental doctrine is identity of the individual soul with the universal soul or *Brahma*.

Vedanta · One of the six orthodox systems of Hindu philosophy, founded on the *Upanishads*. Exposition of the deepest truths of the *Vedas*, which record the experiences of those who gained knowledge of the highest order through intuition and inspiration. Object of existence is realization, not release. Realization not gained through logical inquiry but through direct intuition of inspired sages.

Vedas · The primary scriptures of Hinduism, revered as "not of human origin," eternal, imperishable, and indestructible. Existed in their perfect form from the beginning of time. Revealed by all-knowing *Brahma* to inspired *rishis* of old.

Vishnu · Major god of the Hindu pantheon, forming with *Brahma* and *Siva* the great triad of Hindu deities. *Vishnu* is the preserver, whereas *Siva* is the destroyer. *Krishna* is the most important of the incarnations, or *avatars*, of *Vishnu*.

Vivekananda · Nineteenth century follower of *Ramakrishna*. Established *Ramakrishna Missions* and spread the gospel of reformed Hinduism.

Yoga · One of the six orthodox systems of Hindu philosophy. A code of ascetic disciplines in existence as early as the Indus Valley civilization. Aim is to teach the means by which the human soul may attain union with the universal soul. Several forms of yoga exist. The highest form of *yoga*, often called *raja yoga*, stresses spirituality, not physical culture. A *yogi* is one who practices *yoga*.

Selected Bibliography

Abhishiktananda (Dom Henri Le Saux). *The Further Shore*. Delhi: ISPCK, 1975.

————. *Hindu-Christian Meeting Point*. Revised ed. Delhi: ISPCK, 1976.

————. *Prayer*. Revised ed. Delhi: ISPCK, 1975.

————. *Saccidananda*. Delhi: ISPCK, 1974.

————. *Towards the Renewal of the Indian Church*. Cochin, India; KCM Press, 1970.

Aerthayil, James. "The Hesychast Method of Prayer," *Dharma*, II (1977), 204–16.

Amaladoss, Michael. "Towards an Indian Christian Spirituality," *Religion and Society*, XVI (1969), 6–26.

Amalorpavadoss, D.S., ed. *Ecumenism in Perspective*. Bangalore, India: NBCLC, 1976.

————. "Evangelization and Culture," pp. 61–71; and Zago Marcello, "Evangelization in the Religious Situation in Asia," pp. 72–84, in Norbert Greinacher and Alois Muller, eds., *Evange-*

lization in the World Today. Concilium, No. 114. New York: Seabury Press, 1979.

————. *Praying Seminar*. Bangalore, India: National Biblical, Catechetical and Liturgical Centre, n.d.

The Bhagavadgita. Translated by P. Lal. New Delhi: Orient Paperbacks, 1965.

Bhave, Vinoba. *Talks on the Gita*. London: Allen and Unwin, 1960.

Cuttat, Jacques-Albert. *The Encounter of Religions, a Dialogue between the West and the East*. New York: Desclée Company, 1960.

Fischer, Louis. *The Essential Gandhi*. New York: Vintage Books, 1962.

Gandhi, Mahatma. *My Autobiography, or the Story of My Experiments with Truth*. Ahmedabad, India: Navjivan Press, 1948.

Graham, Aelred. *Contemplative Christianity*. New York: Seabury Press, 1975.

Griffiths, Bede. *Christ in India*. New York: Charles Scribner's Sons, 1965.

————. *The Marriage of East and West*. Springfield, Illinois: Templegate Publishers, 1982.

————. "Mystical Theology in the Indian Church," *Jeevadhara*, IX (1979), 262–78.

————. *Return to the Centre*. London: William Collins Son and Co., Ltd., Fount Paperbacks, 1976.

————. *Vedanta and the Christian Faith*. Los Angeles: The Dawn Horse Press, 1973.

Hoefer, Herbert E., ed. *Debate on Mission*. Madras: Gurukul Lutheran Theological College and Research Institute, 1979.

Howard, Leslie G. *The Expansion of God*. Maryknoll, New York: Orbis Books, 1981.

Indian Spirituality in Action. Christa Prema Seva Ashram. Bombay: Asian Trading Corporation, 1973.

Irudayara, X. and Sundaram, L., eds. *Inter-faith Dialogue in Tiruchirapalli*. Madras: SIGA, 1978. (For private circulation only)

John of the Cross. *The Complete Works of Saint John of the Cross*. P. Silverio de Santa Teresa, tr. E. Allison Peers, ed. 3 Vols. London: Burns, Oates and Washbourne, Ltd., 1933.

Mattam, Joseph. *Land of the Trinity*. Bangalore, India: Theological Publications in India, 1975.

May, Peter. *Banaras and Bethlehem*. Madras: Christian Literature Society, 1959.

Merton, Thomas. *The Asian Journal of Thomas Merton*. New York: New Directions, 1968.

———. *Contemplation in a World of Action*. Garden City, New York: Doubleday Company, 1973.

———. *Contemplative Prayer*. Garden City, New York: Doubleday Company, 1971.

Moffitt, John. *Journey to Gorakhpur*. London: Sheldon Press, 1973.

Panikkar, Raimundo. *The Intra-Religious Dialogue*. New York: Paulist Press, 1978.

———. *The Trinity and the Religious Experience of Man*. Madras: The Christian Literature Society, 1970; New York: Orbis Books, 1975.

———. *The Unknown Christ of Hinduism*. Revised ed. Maryknoll, New York: Orbis Books, 1981.

Philokalia. London: Faber and Faber, 1954.

Prabhavananda, Swami. *The Sermon on the Mount According to Vedanta*. Second Indian ed. Madras: Sri Ramakrishna Math, 1979.

Rayan, Samuel. *The Holy Spirit*. Maryknoll, New York: Orbis Books, 1978.

Staffner, Hans. *The Open Door, A Christian Approach to World Religions*. Bangalore: Asian Trading Corporation, 1978.

Teresa of Avila. *Interior Castle*. E. Allison Peers, ed. Garden City, New York: Doubleday Company, 1972.

Way of the Pilgrim, tr. from the Russian by R.M. French. London: SPCK, 1963.